THE Love Your HEART

Mediterranean

(LowCholesterol)

C·O·O·K·B·O·O·K

by
CAROLE KRUPPA

Surrey Books
Chicago

THE LOVE YOUR HEART MEDITERRANEAN (LOW CHOLESTEROL) COOKBOOK is published by Surrey Books, Inc., 230 E. Ohio St., Suite 120, Chicago, Illinois 60611.

First edition: 1 2 3 4 5

This book is manufactured in the U.S.A.

Library of Congress Cataloging-in-Publication data:

Kruppa, Carole.
    The love your heart Mediterranean low cholesterol cookbook /
by Carole Kruppa.—1st ed.
      300 p.   cm.
      Includes index.
      ISBN 0-940625-52-0 : $12.95
      1. Low-fat diet—Recipes. 2. Low-cholesterol diet—Recipes. 3. Salt-free diet—Recipes. 4. Cookery, Mediterranean. 5. Coronary heart disease—Prevention.
      I. Title.
      RM237.7.K78 1992
      641.5'6311'091822—dc20   92-26761
                                                                                      CIP

Editorial and production: *Bookcrafters, Inc., Chicago*
Art direction: *Hughes & Co., Chicago*
Cover and interior illustrations: *Jean Holabird*

For quantity purchases and prices, contact Surrey Books at the address above.

This title is distributed to the trade by Publishers Group West.

CONTENTS

♥

I dedicate this book to my beautiful grandmother, Senes M. Prespare, who was never too tired or busy to cook for me. She was the kindest, smartest, and most thoughtful person I ever knew—and a wonderful Mediterranean cook.

Vive Meme!

INTRODUCTION

♥

Mediterranean cuisine could be the dream cuisine of the 1990s. It is high in fiber and complex carbohydrates, low in red meats, and extremely flavorful. But what about fat, you might ask? This cuisine has never been shy about pouring on olive oil and spooning in butter and heavy cream. And that brings us directly to the *raison d'être* of this book.

The recipes that follow have been updated and streamlined to reflect today's concern for healthful, nutritious eating. Throughout, we have followed the guidelines set down by the American Heart Association, which call for no more than 30 percent of caloric intake to come from fat. In a few cases that limit has been exceeded; but, remember, the guideline should be applied to one's intake over an entire day, not just to one dish.

Our goal has been to retain the great tastes of Mediterranean cookery while reducing the fat content and controlling calories, cholesterol, and sodium. We hope you'll agree that these recipes succeed in doing just that.

Mediterranean foods are sensuous and hearty. We have tried to retain those characteristics in our reduced-fat versions of these traditional recipes from the South of France, Italy, Greece, Spain, and Morocco. You will find familiar standbys such as ratatouille, risotto, vichyssoise, cioppino, scampi, couscous, flan, and paella. And you will also discover exciting but lesser-known specialties such as caldo de peixe from Morocco, kapama chicken from Greece, fish Basque from Spain, pizza primavera from Italy, and crêpes with raspberry coulis from France.

A few of the recipes from the region will not be found in this collection. There was just no way that we could either reduce fat or substitute ingredients and still maintain the identity of the dish. Thankfully, only a small percentage of traditional Mediterranean cuisine falls into this category.

The people of the Mediterranean tend to be somewhat frugal. Thus, their cuisine uses produce and fruit in season, the bounty of the sea, and native spices and herbs. Large amounts of meat are not the norm. Our recipes follow this lead, making them surprisingly economical yet hearty and satisfying. It is the kind of food you can even diet on painlessly because you never feel starved or deprived.

These Mediterranean recipes use plenty of vegetables, grains, legumes, and fruits, all rich in fiber, vitamins, and minerals. Instead of sodium, we rely mostly on herbs (fresh, if possible) and spices for flavor—the great tastes of cumin, saffron, thyme, basil, cilantro, oregano, the ubiquitous garlic, and a host of others. Instead of butter and cream, we substitute yogurt and evaporated skim milk. We routinely recommend vegetable cooking spray to coat pans and skillets instead of oil. But we haven't eliminated olive oil entirely. We call for it, in moderation, to lend many of these dishes the incomparable flavors for which they are famous. And, remember, olive oil, a monounsaturated vegetable oil, helps stimulate the body's production of HDL, the "good" cholesterol that is thought to inhibit substances that block arteries.

As in my previous collections, *The Love Your Heart Low Cholesterol Cookbook* and *The Free & Equal Cookbooks,* I have attempted to simplify the recipes as much as possible in the interest of saving the cook's time and patience. I have also called mostly for easy-to-obtain ingredients that are found in neighborhood supermarkets at modest prices. Simplicity, convenience, and economy are all values in strict keeping with Mediterranean cookery.

Nutritional data follow each recipe so you'll know how many calories you are eating and the quantities of fat, protein, cholesterol, and sodium you are ingesting. Diabetic exchanges are also given to guide those on more rigorous diets.

Most of us who are charged with the responsibility of cooking for ourselves and our families want meals to be as nourishing and healthful as they are delicious and easy to prepare. We hope these Mediterranean recipes satisfy those criteria. These dishes are the result of centuries of trial and error among the food-loving denizens of southern Europe and northern Africa. Hopefully, we have brought these wonderful foods into harmony with our modern lifestyle and nutritional requirements while retaining all of their lusty taste.

APPETIZERS

FRENCH APPETIZERS

■

MUSHROOMS IN VERMOUTH

1 lb. fresh button mushrooms
½ cup dry vermouth
1 tablespoon olive oil
5 tablespoons red wine vinegar
2 tablespoons lemon juice
1 clove garlic, minced
2 tablespoons shallots, chopped
1 tablespoon fresh basil leaves, chopped
1 teaspoon Spike
½ teaspoon pepper
1 teaspoon sugar
½ teaspoon dry mustard

Place mushrooms into jar with a tight-fitting lid. Combine remaining ingredients in blender and process until smooth. Pour mixture over mushrooms. Seal jar and store in refrigerator for about 2 months.

Serve alone or as a garnish for meats or vegetables.

Serves 6

NUTRITIONAL DATA

PER SERVING		EXCHANGES	
calories	66	milk	0.0
protein (gm)	1.7	vegetable	1.0
fat (gm)	2.6	fruit	0.0

cholesterol (mg)	0	bread	0.0
sodium (mg)	4	meat	0.0
% calories from fat	31	fat	1.0

♥

ASPARAGUS PROVENÇAL

2¼ lbs. asparagus

1 cup diced tomatoes

Vegetable cooking spray

1 yellow pepper, chopped

1 onion, chopped

1 clove garlic, minced

1 teaspoon *herbes de Provençe*

1 recipe Vinaigrette (p. 50)

2 tablespoons fresh parsley, chopped

Trim and dry asparagus. Place asparagus in a steam basket, over boiling water. Steam 6 to 10 minutes. Freshly cut young asparagus cooks quickly, but the fatter spears may take longer. Drain asparagus well, and divide among four hot individual gratin dishes.

Add tomatoes and set aside.

Spray a small skillet with vegetable cooking spray and combine yellow pepper, onion, garlic, and herbs. Cook about 5 minutes. Add to vinaigrette, and pour over asparagus. Top with parsley.

Serves 4

NUTRITIONAL DATA

PER SERVING		EXCHANGES	
calories	106	milk	0.0
protein (gm)	8.1	vegetable	4.0
fat (gm)	1.4	fruit	0.0
cholesterol (mg)	0	bread	0.0
sodium (mg)	22	meat	0.0
% calories from fat	10	fat	0.0

ENDIVE LEAVES WITH RATATOUILLE

Vegetable cooking spray
1 eggplant, cut into ½-in. cubes
1 zucchini, diced
2 tomatoes, diced
1 onion, diced
¼ cup fresh thyme, chopped
3 cloves garlic, minced
Pepper to taste
40 large leaves endive, preferably Belgian

In a large saucepan sprayed with vegetable cooking spray, saute eggplant, zucchini, tomatoes, and onion for 5 minutes. Add thyme, garlic, and pepper. Cover and cook over low heat for 10 minutes.

When cool, spoon vegetable mixture into endive leaves. Arrange filled endive leaves in a fan pattern on a large platter. Makes 40 appetizers.

Serves 20

NUTRITIONAL DATA

PER SERVING		EXCHANGES	
calories	13	milk	0.0
protein (gm)	0.6	vegetable	0.0
fat (gm)	0.1	fruit	0.0
cholesterol (mg)	0	bread	0.0
sodium (mg)	7	meat	0.0
% calories from fat	8	fat	0.0

♥

■

PROVENÇAL ONION TART

This makes an excellent first course, or it can be taken along as part of a picnic meal.

DOUGH

2 cups white bread flour

1 level teaspoon salt

½ oz. fresh yeast, or 1 level teaspoon dried yeast

⅔ cup warm water

1 tablespoon olive oil

FILLING

Vegetable cooking spray

1½ lbs. onions, sliced

2 cloves garlic, minced

1 tablespoon *herbes de Provençe*

4 black olives, sliced

Freshly ground pepper

Herbes de Provençe

Dough: Sift flour and salt into a warm bowl and set aside. Cream the fresh yeast with half the water, or sprinkle the dried yeast onto the water. Leave in a warm place about 10 minutes until frothy. Add yeast mixture to flour with remaining water and oil.

Mix well, then knead 5 minutes until dough feels elastic. Place dough back in bowl, cover with a towel, and leave in a warm place for about 1 hour, or until dough has doubled in size.

Filling: Meanwhile, spray a saucepan with vegetable cooking spray and add onions, garlic, and *herbes de Provençe*. Cover and cook over low heat about 30 minutes until onions are soft but still golden. Remove from heat and cool.

Turn dough out onto a floured circle and place on a greased baking sheet. Spread onion mixture over dough and decorate with olives. Season with pepper and sprinkle *herbes de Provençe* on top lightly.

Leave baking sheet in a warm place about 30 minutes until dough has risen and is slightly puffy. Bake in a 435° oven 25–30 minutes. Serve hot, warm, or cold.

Serves 12

NUTRITIONAL DATA

PER SERVING		EXCHANGES	
calories	113	milk	0.0
protein (gm)	3.4	vegetable	1.0
fat (gm)	1.6	fruit	0.0
cholesterol (mg)	0	bread	1.0
sodium (mg)	186	meat	0.0
% calories from fat	13	fat	0.5

♥

MUSHROOM PÂTÉ

Vegetable cooking spray
2 lbs. mushrooms, finely chopped
¾ teaspoon Spike
Pepper, freshly ground to taste
Egg substitute to equal 3 eggs
1 tablespoon skim milk

Spray 3-cup mold with vegetable cooking spray.

Spray a heavy skillet with vegetable spray and add mushrooms. Cook over low heat, stirring frequently until liquid evaporates and mushrooms brown, about 20 minutes. Season with Spike and pepper. Remove from heat.

In separate bowl, mix egg substitute with skim milk. To this, add 3 tablespoons mushroom mixture. Mix well. Combine egg mixture with mushrooms in skillet. Cook over low heat 2–3 minutes, stirring constantly.

Pour into mold. Chill until firm. Unmold and serve at room temperature with crackers.

Serves 10

NUTRITIONAL DATA

PER SERVING		EXCHANGES	
calories	39	milk	0.0
protein (gm)	4.2	vegetable	1.5
fat (gm)	1.0	fruit	0.0
cholesterol (mg)	0	bread	0.0
sodium (mg)	38	meat	0.0
% calories from fat	21	fat	0.0

♥

VEGETABLE FLAN

1 medium shallot

2 medium carrots

2 medium yellow squash

2 medium zucchini

Egg substitute to equal 4 eggs

1 cup evaporated skim milk

1 teaspoon basil

¼ cup Parmesan cheese, freshly grated

Vegetable cooking spray

2 tablespoons parsley, chopped

Grate vegetables, or shred in food processor. In a 10-in. skillet, bring 2 cups water to boil. Add vegetables and cook until tender. Drain and set aside.

In medium bowl, whisk egg substitute, milk, basil, and ⅛ cup cheese. Add vegetables and mix well. Place mixture in a 13x9-in. baking pan sprayed with vegetable cooking spray. Sprinkle with remaining cheese and parsley. Bake in preheated 350° oven 12–15 minutes or until just set.

Serves 8

NUTRITIONAL DATA

PER SERVING		EXCHANGES	
calories	82	milk	0.5
protein (gm)	7.9	vegetable	1.0
fat (gm)	2.1	fruit	0.0
cholesterol (mg)	4	bread	0.0
sodium (mg)	158	meat	0.5
% calories from fat	23	fat	0.0

ITALIAN APPETIZERS

∎ ANTIPASTO

Following are recipes for roasted peppers with herbs, marinated artichoke hearts and peppers, and dried tomatoes in herb oil. These make a nice addition to raw vegetables, garbanzo beans, cheese, and olives when serving antipasto.

∎ ROASTED PEPPERS WITH HERBS

3 large bell peppers (about 1½ lbs.)
3 large yellow peppers (about 1½ lbs.)
2 large green peppers (about 1 lb.)
1 clove garlic, halved
1 tablespoon olive oil
1 teaspoon Spike
1 tablespoon *herbes de Provençe*

Cut peppers in half lengthwise; discard seeds and membranes. Cut lengthwise into 1-in. strips; set aside.

Rub bottom of a 13 x 9 x 2-in. baking dish with garlic halves; add peppers and oil, tossing well. Bake at 400° for 55 minutes, or until peppers are tender and edges begin to blacken, stirring occasionally.

Combine Spike with *herbes de Provençe;* sprinkle over peppers. Serve warm or cold.

Serves 12

NUTRITIONAL DATA

PER SERVING		EXCHANGES	
calories	14	milk	0.0
protein (gm)	0.5	vegetable	0.0
fat (gm)	0.1	fruit	0.0
cholesterol (mg)	0	bread	0.0
sodium (mg)	1	meat	0.0
% calories from fat	5	fat	0.0

♥

MARINATED ARTICHOKE HEARTS AND PEPPERS

¾ cup water

¼ cup balsamic vinegar

3 teaspoons capers

2 teaspoons Dijon mustard

½ teaspoon dried basil

1 tablespoon fresh parsley, chopped

2 cloves garlic, minced

1 20-oz. can artichoke hearts

1 lb. red and yellow peppers, cut into strips (about 2 large peppers)

4 large black olives, sliced

¼ cup pimiento, diced

½ cup parsley, chopped
Boston lettuce leaves

Combine water, vinegar, capers, mustard, basil, parsley, and garlic in a large bottle with tight-fitting lid. Shake well.

Put artichoke hearts, peppers, olives, pimiento, and parsley into a bowl. Pour dressing over vegetables and mix well.

Arrange lettuce leaves on a platter, and spoon marinated vegetables onto them. Place in refrigerator 2 hours before serving. When ready to serve, place toothpicks alongside platter.

Serves 12

NUTRITIONAL DATA

PER SERVING		EXCHANGES	
calories	43	milk	0.0
protein (gm)	2.2	vegetable	1.5
fat (gm)	0.5	fruit	0.0
cholesterol (mg)	0	bread	0.0
sodium (mg)	66	meat	0.0
% calories from fat	8	fat	0.0

♥

"SUN-DRIED" TOMATOES IN HERB OIL

You can make tomatoes with the unique flavor and characteristic texture of the sun-dried tomatoes sold in gourmet shops. They should sit in the herb oil for at least 4 weeks before using with pasta, salads, pizza, and spreads. They will keep indefinitely if put up correctly in airtight jars. You can also dry the tomatoes on screens or racks in the sun, Italian style, if you live in a dry climate. It will take several days in the hot sun; bring the tomatoes in at night.

6 lbs. ripe Italian plum tomatoes

2 tablespoons Spike

3 3-in. fresh rosemary sprigs

3 garlic cloves, unpeeled

3 3-in. fresh oregano sprigs

8 black peppercorns

3 3-in. thyme sprigs

2½–3 cups olive oil

Preheat oven to 200°. Line baking sheets with racks. Slice open tomatoes lengthwise but not completely in half. Arrange on racks, cut-side up. Sprinkle with Spike.

Bake 12 hours or until tomatoes reduce to about one-fourth their size and appear shriveled and deep red. Remove tomatoes from oven. Cool 1 hour.

Pack into sterilized pint jars (about 14 per pint). Add herbs and cover completely with olive oil. *Seal jar tightly.* Store at room temperature 4–8 weeks before draining and using (see Note).

Makes 3 pints.

Serves 4 per pint

NUTRITIONAL DATA

PER SERVING		EXCHANGES	
calories	56	milk	0.0
protein (gm)	2.0	vegetable	2.0
fat (gm)	1.5	fruit	0.0
cholesterol (mg)	0	bread	0.0
sodium (mg)	20	meat	0.0
% calories from fat	21	fat	0.0

Note: If you are very concerned about reducing fat, rinse the prepared tomatoes in cold water before using.

CAPONATA

¼ cup olive oil

2 onions, thinly sliced

1 garlic clove, minced

1 medium-size tomato, peeled and chopped

2 celery ribs, diced

1 medium eggplant, peeled and diced

1 green pepper, diced

6 black olives, chopped

2 tablespoons red wine vinegar

1 tablespoon sugar

1 teaspoon Spike

¼ teaspoon black pepper, freshly ground

¼ cup capers, drained

Romaine or watercress leaves

1 red bell pepper, thinly sliced for garnish

In 2-qt. microwave casserole, combine oil, onions, and garlic. Cover with lid or vented plastic wrap and microwave on High 2 minutes or until onions are slightly tender. Stir in remaining ingredients except capers, romaine, and red pepper.

Cover and microwave 12 minutes, turning after 6 minutes. Stir in capers. Let stand at room temperature 1 hour. If not serving immediately, refrigerate, then reheat on High 3 to 4 minutes or until warm, stirring once.

To serve, line 6 salad plates with romaine or watercress. Spoon caponata onto lettuce, and fan out red pepper slices at edge of each plate.

Serves 6

NUTRITIONAL DATA

PER SERVING		EXCHANGES	
calories	49	milk	0.0
protein (gm)	1.3	vegetable	2.0

fat (gm)	0.6	fruit	0.0
cholesterol (mg)	0	bread	0.0
sodium (mg)	26	meat	0.0
% calories from fat	10	fat	0.0

♥

Note: Caponata is also delicious as a topping for Bruschetta (see following recipe).

BRUSCHETTA

B ruschetta is the original garlic bread, which can be served as an appetizer or by itself for lunch in much the same way a pizza is served.

12 1-in. slices coarse bread, such as Italian country bread

2 garlic cloves, cut into 1-in. slices

2 tablespoons olive oil (optional)

2 tomatoes, sliced thin

12 fresh basil leaves, chopped

Grill bread over a fire or under broiler until just beginning to brown around edges. It should remain soft inside. Remove from heat and rub while still hot with a cut clove of garlic. Brush with olive oil and top with slice of tomato. Sprinkle with fresh basil.

Serves 12

NUTRITIONAL DATA

PER SERVING		EXCHANGES	
calories	90	milk	0.0
protein (gm)	3.2	vegetable	0.5
fat (gm)	0.1	fruit	0.0
cholesterol (mg)	0	bread	1.0
sodium (mg)	154	meat	0.0
% calories from fat	1	fat	0.0

TOMATOES WITH MOZZARELLA AND BASIL

4 tomatoes

  Lettuce leaves, red preferable

4 tablespoons white wine

1 tablespoon lemon juice

1 teaspoon oregano

4 tablespoons part-skim mozzarella cheese, shredded

8 large fresh basil leaves

Cut tomatoes into slices and arrange on 4 individual salad plates with lettuce leaves. Blend wine, lemon juice, and oregano. Drizzle over tomatoes. Sprinkle on 1 tablespoon cheese. Top with fresh basil leaves.

  Serves 4

NUTRITIONAL DATA

PER SERVING		EXCHANGES	
calories	72	milk	0.0
protein (gm)	4.5	vegetable	1.0
fat (gm)	2.7	fruit	0.0
cholesterol (mg)	8	bread	0.0
sodium (mg)	78	meat	0.5
% calories from fat	31	fat	0.5

♥

GREEK APPETIZERS

CHESTNUT AND CHICKEN CANAPÉS

This unusual recipe is perfect for afternoon receptions and with champagne.

12 chestnuts, fresh or dried

2 cups cooked chicken breast meat, ground or finely minced

¼ cup celery, finely chopped

¼ cup pimiento, chopped

½ cup Mock Sour Cream (p. 232)

1 teaspoon Spike

1 teaspoon white pepper

Assorted breads, plain or toasted

Cut an "X" in flat side of each chestnut shell with small, sharp knife. Cover nuts with water, bring to boil, and simmer 45 minutes to 1 hour, covered. Drain, and while still hot, peel chestnuts. (If you use the dried, shelled chestnuts available at ethnic grocery stores, soak them in warm water 1–2 days; then simmer, drain, and use.)

In a blender, mix chestnuts, chicken, celery, pimiento, mock sour cream, Spike, and white pepper. Process until smooth. Refrigerate until cold. (If you do not want a pureed spread, combine in a bowl instead of using blender.)

Using a sharp knife, cut crust off breads. With cookie cutters, cut bread into various shapes. Wrap tightly in plastic wrap and refrigerate. Before serving, spread bread with cold chestnut and chicken mixture.

Makes about 3 cups of spread, or 48 tablespoons.

Serves 12 (4 tablespoons per serving)

NUTRITIONAL DATA

PER SERVING		EXCHANGES	
calories	140	milk	0.0
protein (gm)	8.5	vegetable	0.0
fat (gm)	4.3	fruit	0.0
cholesterol (mg)	16	bread	1.0
sodium (mg)	134	meat	1.0
% calories from fat	25	fat	0.5

♥

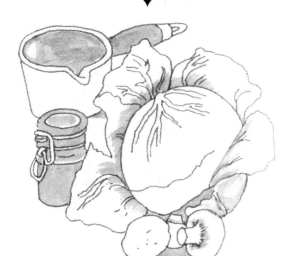

HUMMUS

2 16-oz. cans garbanzo beans

Juice from 1 lemon

4 cloves garlic, minced

2 tablespoons olive oil

¼ cup fresh parsley, chopped

Drain the juice from 1 can garbanzo beans. Place drained beans in blender or processor, then add the second can of beans, water and all. Add lemon juice and garlic, and blend until very smooth.

Pour into a bowl or onto a large plate with a lip. Pour olive oil over the top. Sprinkle with parsley.

Serve alone or with bread and crackers or raw vegetables.

Serves 10

NUTRITIONAL DATA

PER SERVING		EXCHANGES	
calories	115	milk	0.0
protein (gm)	4.3	vegetable	0.0
fat (gm)	4.3	fruit	0.0
cholesterol (mg)	0	bread	1.0
sodium (mg)	362	meat	0.0
% calories from fat	33	fat	1.0

♥

SPANISH APPETIZERS

MUSSELS IN SPICY SAUCE

3 cups canned mussels, drained

6 tablespoons low-fat mayonnaise

6 teaspoons mustard

3 teaspoons sherry

1½ teaspoons lemon juice

3 2½-oz. jars pimiento, chopped

Place mussels on platter. Combine remaining ingredients. Spoon sauce over mussels.

Serves 6

NUTRITIONAL DATA

PER SERVING		EXCHANGES	
calories	126	milk	0.0
protein (gm)	11.0	vegetable	0.0
fat (gm)	5.8	fruit	0.0
cholesterol (mg)	47	bread	0.0
sodium (mg)	283	meat	1.5
% calories from fat	28	fat	1.0

ARTICHOKES WITH GREEN SAUCE

1 8½-oz. can artichoke hearts

4 tablespoons white wine

2 tablespoons lemon juice

1 tablespoon parsley, finely chopped

½ teaspoon marjoram

¼ teaspoon tarragon

Drain artichoke hearts. Combine wine, lemon juice, and herbs. Pour mixture over artichoke hearts.

Serves 4

NUTRITIONAL DATA

PER SERVING		EXCHANGES	
calories	39	milk	0.0
protein (gm)	2.0	vegetable	1.5
fat (gm)	0.2	fruit	0.0
cholesterol (mg)	0	bread	0.0
sodium (mg)	55	meat	0.0
% calories from fat	4	fat	0.0

♥

ARTICHOKE DIP

28 ozs. canned artichokes, drained and chopped

½ cup Mock Sour Cream (p. 232)

2 cups low-fat cottage cheese, whipped until smooth

½ cup Parmesan cheese, grated

3 tablespoons scallions, chopped

2 tablespoons chives, chopped

4 tablespoons Marsala wine

In small bowl, combine all ingredients. Mix well. Spoon mixture into a greased casserole. Bake in preheated 375° oven 30 minutes or until golden brown. Serve immediately with crackers, vegetables, or black bread.

Serves 10

NUTRITIONAL DATA

PER SERVING		EXCHANGES	
calories	113	milk	0.0
protein (gm)	11.7	vegetable	1.5
fat (gm)	2.7	fruit	0.0
cholesterol (mg)	8	bread	0.0
sodium (mg)	365	meat	1.5
% calories from fat	20	fat	0.0

♥

MOROCCAN APPETIZERS

☆

EGGPLANT SALAD

2 medium eggplants
Spike
Vegetable cooking spray
4 cloves garlic, minced
1 tablespoon sharp paprika
1 teaspoon cumin, ground
1 tablespoon olive oil
2 tablespoons vinegar or lemon juice

Remove 3 vertical strips of skin from each eggplant, leaving it striped, then cut eggplant into ½-in.-thick slices. Sprinkle with Spike and leave to drain in colander 30 minutes. Rinse well, squeeze gently, and pat dry with paper towels.

Place a skillet on medium-high heat, and spray with vegetable cooking spray. Saute eggplant slices a few at a time over high heat until golden brown on both sides. Drain.

Mash eggplant with garlic and spices. Saute this puree in olive oil in same skillet until all liquid evaporates and there is only vegetable left. Stir puree often to avoid scorching. Pour off any oil, and season with vinegar or lemon juice to taste.

Serve at room temperature with pita bread or crackers.

Serves 8

NUTRITIONAL DATA

PER SERVING		EXCHANGES	
calories	32	milk	0.0
protein (gm)	0.9	vegetable	1.0
fat (gm)	0.3	fruit	0.0
cholesterol (mg)	0	bread	0.0
sodium (mg)	8	meat	0.0
% calories from fat	7	fat	0.0

SOUPS

FRENCH SOUPS

FRENCH ONION SOUP

1 lb. onions

Vegetable cooking spray

Pepper

½ teaspoon mustard

2 teaspoons plain flour

4 cups beef stock (homemade or low-sodium canned)

1 cup white wine

4-6 slices French bread, lightly toasted

1 oz. (¼ cup) Parmesan cheese, freshly grated

Peel and finely slice onions. Spray a large skillet with vegetable cooking spray, then add onion rings, pepper, and mustard. Cook over a very gentle heat, stirring occasionally until onion is browned (this will take 20–30 minutes).

Add flour and stir until smooth. Add stock and white wine, stirring constantly, then bring to boil and simmer 30 minutes. Taste and adjust seasoning.

Place slices of toasted bread on bottom of a soup tureen or in individual soup bowls, sprinkling with cheese. Pour hot soup carefully onto bread. Place under the broiler until cheese is beginning to brown. Serve immediately.

Serves 6

NUTRITIONAL DATA

PER SERVING		EXCHANGES	
calories	167	milk	0.0
protein (gm)	6.8	vegetable	2.0
fat (gm)	3.5	fruit	0.0
cholesterol (mg)	6	bread	1.0
sodium (mg)	263	meat	0.5
% calories from fat	19	fat	0.5

♥

VICHYSSOISE
(Cold Leek Soup)

Vegetable cooking spray

4 leeks (white part only)

1 onion

2 shallots

6¼ cups chicken stock (homemade or low-sodium canned)

1 lb. potatoes

1 cup evaporated skim milk

1 tablespoon chives, snipped

Nutmeg, pinch

Pepper to taste

Prepare vegetables by slicing thinly. Spray a large skillet with vegetable cooking spray, then add leeks, onion, and shallots. Saute, stirring until softened. Add stock and potatoes, bring to boil, cover pan, and simmer 30–40 minutes.

Press soup through a sieve with wooden spoon, or puree in blender. Refrigerate until quite cold. Stir in evaporated skim milk and chives. Season with nutmeg and pepper to taste. Add a little extra stock if soup is too thick.

Serve cold in chilled soup cups, or heat to serve warm if you prefer.

Serves 6

NUTRITIONAL DATA

PER SERVING		EXCHANGES	
calories	190	milk	0.5
protein (gm)	8.5	vegetable	2.0
fat (gm)	2.1	fruit	0.0
cholesterol (mg)	6	bread	1.0
sodium (mg)	126	meat	0.0
% calories from fat	10	fat	0.5

♥

WHITE BEAN SOUP PROVENÇALE

2 tablespoons light olive oil

1 cup each, celery and onion, chopped

3 cloves garlic

2 teaspoons dried sage

6 cups chicken stock (divided)

2 cups water

1 lb. dried navy beans

2 teaspoons fresh lemon juice

Spike

Pepper, freshly ground

Garnish:

3 large plum tomatoes, chopped

¼ cup fresh basil leaves, cut julienne

Heat oil in 4-qt. saucepan or stockpot. When hot, add celery, onion, garlic, and sage. Cook until onion is softened, about 5 minutes. Add 5 cups stock and water. Heat to boil. Add beans. Heat to boil again. Reduce heat; simmer covered 2 hours, stirring occasionally.

Remove 2 cups bean mixture and puree with 1 cup reserved stock in food processor or blender until smooth. Return pureed mixture to pot. Stir well to combine. Add lemon juice and seasonings to taste.

This soup can be made ahead and frozen or refrigerated as long as 3 days. Reheat gently, thinning with water as needed. Adjust seasonings and lemon juice. To serve, garnish with tomato and basil.

Serves 10

NUTRITIONAL DATA

PER SERVING		EXCHANGES	
calories	210	milk	0.0
protein (gm)	12.6	vegetable	1.0
fat (gm)	4.3	fruit	0.0
cholesterol (mg)	0	bread	2.0
sodium (mg)	471	meat	0.0
% calories from fat	18	fat	1.0

♥

■

LENTIL SOUP

Vegetable cooking spray

1 leek, well rinsed and finely minced

1 carrot, finely minced

1 onion, finely minced

1 celery rib, finely minced

1 teaspoon ground cumin

4 whole cloves garlic

1 lb. imported green lentils

2 bay leaves

Black pepper, freshly ground

Spray a large stockpot with vegetable cooking spray, and add minced vegetables, cumin, and garlic; saute until all are nicely browned. Add lentils, bay leaves, and pepper to taste. Stir in 2½ qts. water and simmer, covered, until lentils are cooked through, about 45 minutes.

Serves 8

NUTRITIONAL DATA

PER SERVING		EXCHANGES	
calories	225	milk	0.0
protein (gm)	15.7	vegetable	1.0
fat (gm)	1.5	fruit	0.0
cholesterol (mg)	0	bread	2.0
sodium (mg)	456	meat	1.0
% calories from fat	6	fat	0.0

♥

ITALIAN SOUPS

MINESTRONE

2 teaspoons olive oil

1 medium-size onion, finely chopped

1 garlic clove, minced

4 cups salt-free vegetable stock, or 2 salt-free vegetable bouillon cubes or packets reconstituted with 4 cups water (divided)

1 cup white wine

1 15½-oz. can chunky tomatoes

2 cups cooked garbanzo beans, or canned garbanzo beans, well drained

1 large celery stalk, diced

1 medium-size carrot, thinly sliced

1 large boiling potato, peeled, cut into ¾-in. cubes

1 medium zucchini, diced

¼ cup fresh parsley leaves, chopped

1 teaspoon dried basil leaves

½ teaspoon dried marjoram leaves

¼ teaspoon dried thyme leaves

¼ teaspoon black pepper

½ cup small pasta seashells or macaroni, uncooked

Spike to taste

In a stockpot, combine olive oil, onion, garlic, and 3 tablespoons vegetable stock. Cook over medium-high heat, stirring frequently,

5–6 minutes until onion is tender. If liquid begins to evaporate, add a bit more stock.

Add remaining vegetable stock, wine, tomatoes, garbanzo beans, celery, carrot, potato, and zucchini. Then add remaining ingredients except pasta and Spike. Stir to mix well. Cover and bring to boil. Lower heat and simmer about 15 minutes.

Bring soup to boil again. Add pasta. Lower heat again and simmer, stirring occasionally, an additional 15–20 minutes until vegetables and pasta are tender. Add Spike to taste. As pasta thickens soup, stir to make sure it doesn't stick to bottom of pot.

This soup is best the day it's made since pasta tends to absorb liquid. When reheating, add a bit more vegetable stock or bouillon.

Serves 6

NUTRITIONAL DATA

PER SERVING		EXCHANGES	
calories	265	milk	0.0
protein (gm)	11.3	vegetable	3.0
fat (gm)	4.5	fruit	0.0
cholesterol (mg)	2	bread	2.0
sodium (mg)	180	meat	0.0
% calories from fat	15	fat	1.0

♥

GARLIC SOUP

6 cups water

3 tablespoons tomato paste

18 cloves garlic, crushed

1 cup Italian parsley, chopped

1 tablespoon Italian seasoning

1 bay leaf

4 slices hard-crusted Italian bread

½ cup Parmesan cheese, freshly grated

Boil water. Add all ingredients, except Parmesan cheese and bread. Simmer 15 minutes.

Toast bread and sprinkle it with cheese. Place one piece of bread in each of 4 bowls. Cover with soup.

Serves 4

NUTRITIONAL DATA

PER SERVING		EXCHANGES	
calories	178	milk	0.0
protein (gm)	9.9	vegetable	2.0
fat (gm)	4.0	fruit	0.0
cholesterol (mg)	10	bread	1.0
sodium (mg)	490	meat	1.0
% calories from fat	21	fat	0.0

♥

ITALIAN MUSHROOM SOUP

This is a very sophisticated soup that is ideal for formal dinner parties.

Vegetable cooking spray

2 medium onions, chopped

1 lb. fresh mushrooms, thinly sliced (see Note)

6 tablespoons rich tomato puree, or 3 tablespoons tomato paste

4 cups chicken stock or broth (homemade or low-sodium canned)

6 tablespoons sweet vermouth

Spike to taste

1 tablespoon fresh basil, minced

¼ cup chives, minced

Parmesan cheese, freshly grated (optional)

Spray a heavy saucepan with vegetable cooking spray and add onions. Cook until onions are translucent. Add mushrooms and cook until they are softened. Stir in tomato puree and chicken stock. Heat to boiling, then reduce heat and stir in vermouth. Season to taste with Spike. Simmer a few minutes.

Serve hot, sprinkled with basil and chives. You can also top with a dash of Parmesan cheese if you like.

Serves 4

NUTRITIONAL DATA

PER SERVING		EXCHANGES	
calories	128	milk	0.0
protein (gm)	5.8	vegetable	4.0
fat (gm)	2.2	fruit	0.0
cholesterol (mg)	4	bread	0.0
sodium (mg)	154	meat	0.0
% calories from fat	14	fat	0.5

♥

Note: You can make this soup with white cultivated mushrooms, Italian brown field mushrooms or a combination of fresh chanterelles and cultivated mushrooms.

HEARTY FISH SOUP OR RED CLAM CHOWDER

This soup makes a hearty meal when served with crusty bread; a fruit dessert completes the meal. See the "Note" below to convert recipe to clam chowder.

Vegetable cooking spray

2 celery stalks, chopped

2 carrots, sliced

1 green pepper, chopped

1 44-oz. can low-sodium tomatoes

1 6-oz. bottle clam juice

3 medium potatoes, peeled and diced

½ teaspoon black pepper, freshly ground

1 teaspoon oregano

6 fresh basil leaves, torn up

½ lb. fillet of sole, cut into bite-size pieces

½ lb. flounder, cut into bite-size pieces

½ lb. orange roughy, cut into bite-size pieces

1 cup dry white wine

6 tablespoons fresh parsley, chopped

6 fresh basil leaves, chopped, for garnish

Spray a large stockpot with vegetable cooking spray. Add onion, celery, carrots, and green pepper. Cook until just *al dente.* Add tomatoes, clam juice, and potatoes. Cook over medium heat 5 minutes. Add pepper, oregano, and basil. Cover and simmer 20 minutes or until potatoes are done.

Add fish and wine, cover, and continue simmering 10 minutes. Sprinkle with chopped parsley and add additional basil before serving.

Serves 8

NUTRITIONAL DATA

PER SERVING		EXCHANGES	
calories	206	milk	0.0
protein (gm)	21.3	vegetable	3.0
fat (gm)	1.7	fruit	0.0
cholesterol (mg)	52	bread	0.5
sodium (mg)	205	meat	1.5
% calories from fat	7	fat	0.0

Note: To make clam chowder, substitute 6 10-oz. cans minced clams or 4 lbs. fresh clams for the fish. Add clams just before serving.

GREEK SOUPS

KAKAVIA

What the French call bouillabaisse the Greeks call kakavia. This is a favorite party recipe because it feeds a crowd and can be made in advance.

4-6 lbs. whole cleaned fish: striped bass, sea bass, or red snapper

Vegetable cooking spray

4 cups onion, chopped

2 stalks celery, cubed

1 tablespoon garlic, minced

2 leeks, sliced

3 large carrots, pared and cubed

1 tablespoon Spike

1 tablespoon pepper

3 tablespoons fresh lemon juice

1 1-lb. can plum tomatoes with liquid

4 cups water

12 clams, scrubbed

12 shrimps, shelled and deveined

12 mussels, scrubbed and cleaned

1 cup white wine

3 bay leaves

½ teaspoon dried thyme

1 tablespoon parsley, minced

Cut fish into small pieces. Spray a large stockpot with vegetable cooking spray. Saute onion, celery, garlic, and leeks over medium heat 5 minutes. Add carrots, Spike, pepper, lemon juice, tomatoes, and water.

Add seafood (see Note) and remaining ingredients. Cook 15 minutes or until clams and mussels open. Serve in deep bowls with crusty garlic bread.

Serves 12

NUTRITIONAL DATA

PER SERVING		EXCHANGES	
calories	288	milk	0.0
protein (gm)	41.3	vegetable	2.0
fat (gm)	5.0	fruit	0.0
cholesterol (mg)	99	bread	0.0
sodium (mg)	314	meat	4.5
% calories from fat	16	fat	0.0

Note: Baby lobster tails (about ½ lb. each) can be added with other shellfish.

CUCUMBER YOGURT SOUP

The Greeks love yogurt, which is the basis of this delicious and refreshing soup.

3 cups yogurt

1½ cups cucumber, peeled, seeded, and grated

1 teaspoon Spike

¾ cup cold water

1 teaspoon white pepper

1 tablespoon dill, minced

3 tablespoons chives, minced

1 tablespoon garlic, minced

4 thin slices cucumber

Put all ingredients, except cucumber slices, in mixing bowl. Stir until blended. Chill well. Serve in chilled bowls and top each with a cucumber slice. Serve with garlic bread.

Serves 4

NUTRITIONAL DATA

PER SERVING		EXCHANGES	
calories	113	milk	1.0
protein (gm)	9.1	vegetable	0.0
fat (gm)	2.7	fruit	0.0
cholesterol (mg)	10	bread	0.0
sodium (mg)	120	meat	0.0
% calories from fat	21	fat	0.5

Spanish Soups

15-Minute Soup

So many dishes take a long time to prepare and cook, so when a good dish comes along that only takes 15 minutes, it is time to rejoice. The ingredients may vary but the soup is always delicious.

    Vegetable cooking spray
½ medium onion, finely chopped
 2 cloves garlic, chopped
 4 thin slices day-old bread
 2 medium tomatoes, peeled, seeded, and finely
    chopped
 3 cups low-sodium fish stock or clam juice
 3 cups water
    Pepper, freshly ground
 1 teaspoon paprika
½ cup dry sherry
24 clams or mussels in the shell, cleaned
 2 tablespoons parsley, finely chopped, for garnish

Spray a casserole with vegetable cooking spray, and saute onion until soft. Add garlic and bread and saute for a few minutes longer. Add tomatoes and saute briefly, stirring. Stir in fish stock or clam juice and water, and season to taste with pepper. Add paprika, sherry, and clams or mussels.

Cook, covered, just until clams or mussels open, about 5 minutes. Total cooking time should add up to 15 minutes. Garnish soup with parsley. Serve with crusty bread and dry white wine.

Variations: Use rice, about 3 tablespoons, instead of bread. Vegetables such as green peas can also be added. You may also substitute ½ lb. medium prawns (shrimp), peeled and halved, for clams or mussels if you like.

Serves 6

NUTRITIONAL DATA

PER SERVING		EXCHANGES	
calories	142	milk	0.0
protein (gm)	10.3	vegetable	0.0
fat (gm)	2.1	fruit	0.0
cholesterol (mg)	20	bread	1.0
sodium (mg)	179	meat	1.5
% calories from fat	13	fat	0.0

CIOPPINO MEDITERRANEAN

¼ cup green pepper, chopped

2 tablespoons onion, finely chopped

1 clove garlic, minced

1 tablespoon olive oil

2 16-oz. cans tomatoes, chopped

1 6-oz. can low-sodium tomato paste mixed with 1
cup water

½ cup dry red wine

3 tablespoons parsley, snipped

½ teaspoon Spike

1 teaspoon oregano, crushed

1 teaspoon basil, crushed

Pepper, dash

1 lb. fillet of sole

1 lb. shrimp, cleaned and deveined

1 7½-oz. can minced clams

In large saucepan, saute green pepper, onion, and garlic in oil until tender but not brown. Add undrained tomatoes, tomato paste, wine, parsley, Spike, oregano, basil, and dash pepper. Bring to boil. Reduce heat; cover and simmer 20 minutes.

Cut fish fillets into pieces, removing bones. Add fish to broth; simmer 5 minutes. Add shrimp and undrained clams. Continue simmering, covered, about 5 minutes longer.

Serves 6

NUTRITIONAL DATA

PER SERVING		EXCHANGES	
calories	196	milk	0.0
protein (gm)	27.1	vegetable	1.0
fat (gm)	4.1	fruit	0.0
cholesterol (mg)	152	bread	0.0
sodium (mg)	294	meat	3.0
% calories from fat	19	fat	0.0

MOROCCAN SOUP

☆

CALDO DE PEIXE
(Fish Soup)

This dish is meant to be served with rice. If you prefer less carbohydrates and more fish per person, you may wish to double the recipe.

1 teaspoon Spike

2–3 green (unripe) bananas, sliced in rounds

1 yellow onion, sliced

2 tablespoons olive oil

2 cloves garlic, minced

1 bay leaf

1 chili pepper, or ½ teaspoon cayenne pepper

1 bunch parsley, finely chopped

2 large tomatoes, chopped

4 cups hot water

¼ cup tapioca flour (see Note)

¼ cup dry breadcrumbs

½ small cabbage, chopped

4–6 large potatoes, chopped in chunks

4–6 sweet potatoes, chopped in chunks

2 lbs. fish, without bones: flounder, salmon, orange roughy, halibut

Place Spike in mixing bowl and add bananas. Pour in enough water to cover banana pieces. Soak 10–15 minutes to draw out the "pucker" quality of the unripe fruit.

In a deep skillet, brown onion in oil over moderate heat. Add garlic, bay leaf, chili pepper, parsley, and tomatoes, and saute for several minutes, stirring frequently. Stir in 4 cups hot water.

In a separate bowl, use a bit of the hot broth to whisk tapioca flour into a thin, smooth paste. Bring soup in skillet almost to a boil, and add paste and breadcrumbs, stirring vigorously. Immediately reduce heat to simmer.

Drain bananas and add them to skillet along with cabbage and potatoes. Gently lay in fish, cover with water, and simmer 20–30 minutes or until everything is cooked.

Serves 8

NUTRITIONAL DATA

PER SERVING		EXCHANGES	
calories	332	milk	0.0
protein (gm)	23.5	vegetable	1.0
fat (gm)	5.3	fruit	0.5
cholesterol (mg)	53	bread	2.0
sodium (mg)	132	meat	2.0
% calories from fat	14	fat	0.5

Note: If you can't find tapioca flour, substitute quick-cooking, or "minute," tapioca.

SALADS &
SALAD DRESSINGS

FRENCH SALADS & DRESSINGS

■

SALAD NIÇOISE

This salad, unlike the American version, does not contain any boiled vegetables. You will love it.

1 garlic clove
1 large cucumber, peeled and thinly sliced
½ lb. very young string beans
1 green pepper, thinly sliced
1 red pepper, thinly sliced
3 anchovy fillets, cut into pieces
1 8-oz. can tuna, flaked
6 large black olives, sliced
1 recipe Vinaigrette (p. 50)
3 hard-boiled egg whites
1 hard-boiled egg yolk
2 tablespoons parsley, minced

Cut garlic clove in half and rub inside of salad bowl well. Arrange all ingredients, except eggs and parsley, decoratively in bowl. Pour on vinaigrette. Using a fork, mash egg whites and egg yolk together. Sprinkle over salad. Top with parsley.
Serves 6

NUTRITIONAL DATA

PER SERVING		EXCHANGES	
calories	101	milk	0.0
protein (gm)	13.5	vegetable	1.0
fat (gm)	3.0	fruit	0.0
cholesterol (mg)	37	bread	0.0
sodium (mg)	155	meat	1.5
% calories from fat	24	fat	0.0

♥

ASPARAGUS VINAIGRETTE

*Y*ou can use any variety of asparagus for this recipe, but make sure that the stalks are not woody.

> 2 lbs. asparagus
>
> Spike
>
> White pepper
>
> 1 recipe Vinaigrette (p. 50)
>
> Small bunch parsley, finely chopped

Trim any tough or dry ends from asparagus. Steam 8–10 minutes, depending on size of stalks. Larger stalks may take more time. You should be able to pierce stalks with a pointed knife.

Lift out asparagus and drain well. Serve asparagus with dash of Spike and pepper, with vinaigrette poured over and sprinkled with parsley.

Serves 6

NUTRITIONAL DATA

PER SERVING		EXCHANGES	
calories	39	milk	0.0
protein (gm)	3.9	vegetable	1.5
fat (gm)	0.6	fruit	0.0

cholesterol (mg)	0	bread	0.0
sodium (mg)	7	meat	0.0
% calories from fat	11	fat	0.0

TANTE MARIE'S TOSSED GREEN SALAD

2 heads soft leaf or butterhead lettuce, such as Boston, Bibb, or buttercrunch, washed and dried

1 recipe Vinaigrette (see p. 50)

1 cup garlic croutons

Tear greens into bite-size pieces and place in bowl. Pour on vinaigrette. Top with croutons.

Serves 8

NUTRITIONAL DATA

PER SERVING		EXCHANGES	
calories	31	milk	0.0
protein (gm)	1.9	vegetable	0.0
fat (gm)	0.3	fruit	0.0
cholesterol (mg)	0	bread	0.5
sodium (mg)	59	meat	0.0
% calories from fat	10	fat	0.0

Note: Which salad ingredients are used depends on what is available. The following ingredients are all suitable: lettuce, endive, chicory, watercress, dandelion leaves, sorrel, celery, celeriac, cucumber, and green pepper. Fresh herbs are also frequently added, giving a really individual flavor to your salad. You can try any of the following: parsley, chives, lovage, chervil, and mint.

Use just enough vinaigrette sauce to make each individual leaf glisten. The salad should not be sitting in a puddle of dressing.

Serve your salad as soon as it has been tossed or else it may become soggy. For variety, choose another type of dressing such as Tomato Vinaigrette (p. 62) or Balsamic Dressing (p. 61)—be daring!

LEMON, CUCUMBER, AND BELL PEPPER SALAD

2 or 3 lemons (depending on size)

Spike

1 red pepper

1 yellow pepper

2 cucumbers, preferably seedless

1 recipe Creamy Dijon Dressing (p. 52)

1 tablespoon capers

Black pepper, freshly ground

1 tablespoon parsley, chopped

Wash lemons and slice them, with rind on, as thin as possible but no thicker than ⅛ in. With top of paring knife, pick out all seeds. Put lemon slices in small bowl and sprinkle liberally with Spike.

Cut bell peppers lengthwise along creases. Remove stem, core, and seeds. Cut flesh into thinnest possible strips, no more than ¼ in. thick. Set aside.

Using a mandolin, or the single long slit of a four-sided grater, or the thin slicing disk of a food processor, slice cucumbers paper-thin, leaving peel on. Set sliced cucumber aside.

When ready to assemble, choose a very shallow bowl, in which ingredients can be fanned out. Line bottom with cucumber slices. Drain lemon and put slices over cucumber, allowing a border of cucumber to show. Repeat this concentric arrangement with peppers, placing them over lemon slices.

Pour dressing over in a figure 8 pattern to distribute it evenly. Add capers and fresh pepper, and top with chopped parsley. Just before serving, sprinkle with Spike.

Serves 6

NUTRITIONAL DATA

PER SERVING		EXCHANGES	
calories	33	milk	0.0
protein (gm)	2.0	vegetable	1.5
fat (gm)	0.3	fruit	0.0
cholesterol (mg)	0	bread	0.0
sodium (mg)	35	meat	0.0
% calories from fat	8	fat	0.0

♥

FRENCH VINAIGRETTE

¾ cup water

2 garlic cloves, minced

¼ cup wine vinegar

3 teaspoons capers

2 teaspoons Dijon mustard

1 teaspoon tarragon

1 teaspoon thyme

1 teaspoon fresh purple (or regular) basil, chopped

1 tablespoon fresh parsley, chopped

Combine ingredients. Adjust vinegar to taste. Store in covered container.

Makes about 1 cup.

Serves 16 (1 tablespoon per serving)

NUTRITIONAL DATA

PER SERVING		EXCHANGES	
calories	1	milk	0.0
protein (gm)	0.0	vegetable	0.0
fat (gm)	0.0	fruit	0.0
cholesterol (mg)	0	bread	0.0
sodium (mg)	9	meat	0.0
% calories from fat	2	fat	0.0

CREAMY ONION DRESSING

½ cup plain, non-fat yogurt

1½ teaspoons Dijon mustard

2 tablespoons dried onion, minced

½ small scallion, minced

2 teaspoons fresh chives, minced

Dash black pepper, fresh ground

Combine all ingredients in blender. Process until smooth.
Makes about ½ cup.
Serves 8 (1 tablespoon per serving)

NUTRITIONAL DATA

PER SERVING		EXCHANGES	
calories	12	milk	0.0
protein (gm)	0.9	vegetable	0.0
fat (gm)	0.0	fruit	0.0
cholesterol (mg)	0	bread	0.0
sodium (mg)	11	meat	0.0
% calories from fat	2	fat	0.0

CREAMY DIJON DRESSING

1 cup low-fat cottage cheese

4 tablespoons skim milk

3 teaspoons Dijon mustard

3 teaspoons lemon juice

2 tablespoons chives, minced

Combine all ingredients in blender. Process until smooth.
Makes about ½ cup.
Serves 8 (1 tablespoon per serving)

NUTRITIONAL DATA

PER SERVING		EXCHANGES	
calories	10	milk	0.0
protein (gm)	0.9	vegetable	0.0
fat (gm)	0.1	fruit	0.0
cholesterol (mg)	0	bread	0.0
sodium (mg)	24	meat	0.0
% calories from fat	8	fat	0.0

ITALIAN SALADS & DRESSINGS

MUSHROOM SALAD

1 recipe Italian Dressing (p. 55)

1 lb. fresh mushrooms, sliced thin (use caps only); if available, mix 2 or 3 different varieties of mushrooms

1 head romaine lettuce, torn into pieces

1 large yellow pepper

Black pepper to taste

Place all ingredients in a bowl and mix well.
Serves 8

NUTRITIONAL DATA

PER SERVING		EXCHANGES	
calories	27	milk	0.0
protein (gm)	1.6	vegetable	1.0
fat (gm)	0.3	fruit	0.0
cholesterol (mg)	0	bread	0.0
sodium (mg)	4	meat	0.0
% calories from fat	8	fat	0.0

SEAFOOD PASTA SALAD

This is easy, fast, and a people pleaser. It can be prepared ahead of time and is great for a buffet.

1 lb. asparagus

1 lb. shrimp, peeled and deveined

1 lb. scallops

2 lbs. pasta shells

1 cup fresh basil leaves

1 garlic clove, minced

½ basket cherry tomatoes

1 recipe Vinaigrette (p. 50)

½ cup Parmesan cheese, freshly grated

6 fresh basil leaves for garnish

Cut woody ends from asparagus and steam 8–10 minutes. Set aside.

Boil shrimp and scallops 3–4 minutes, until just cooked. Drain and let cool.

Cook pasta shells until *al dente* (see Note), drain, and let cool. Toss all ingredients together with basil, garlic, and tomatoes. Pour on vinaigrette. Add cheese, and garnish with basil leaves.

Serves 10

NUTRITIONAL DATA

PER SERVING		EXCHANGES	
calories	409	milk	0.0
protein (gm)	28.2	vegetable	1.0
fat (gm)	4.2	fruit	0.0
cholesterol (mg)	162	bread	3.0
sodium (mg)	204	meat	3.0
% calories from fat	9	fat	0.0

Note: *Al dente* means firm to the tooth, not mushy.

ITALIAN DRESSING

¼ cup lemon juice
¼ cup red wine vinegar
¼ cup white wine
1 teaspoon oregano
1 teaspoon basil
½ teaspoon dry mustard
½ teaspoon onion powder
1 clove garlic, minced
1 tablespoon chives, chopped
1 teaspoon thyme
½ teaspoon rosemary

Combine all ingredients. Chill for an hour or two to allow herbs to blend.

Makes ¾ cup.

Serves 12 (1 tablespoon per serving)

NUTRITIONAL DATA

PER SERVING		EXCHANGES	
calories	5	milk	0.0
protein (gm)	0.0	vegetable	0.0
fat (gm)	0.0	fruit	0.0
cholesterol (mg)	0	bread	0.0
sodium (mg)	0	meat	0.0
% calories from fat	0	fat	0.0

GREEK SALADS & DRESSINGS

CLASSIC GREEK SALAD

*A nyone who has been to Greece in the summer
will remember the luscious tomatoes served
everywhere.*

> 4 plump tomatoes, cored and quartered
> 1 cucumber, peeled and cut into ¼-in. slices
> 1 green pepper, seeded and cut into thin, round slices
> 1 yellow pepper, seeded and cut into thin, round slices
> 1 red pepper, seeded and cut into thin, round slices
> 2-3 anchovies (optional)
> 12 black olives
> 1 large red onion, peeled and cut into thin slices
> ¼ cup feta cheese, crumbled
> 1 recipe Vinaigrette (p. 50)

Combine tomatoes, cucumber, peppers, anchovies, olives, onions, and feta cheese in a medium-size bowl. Pour on vinaigrette. Toss once more just before serving.
  Serves 6

NUTRITIONAL DATA

PER SERVING		EXCHANGES	
calories	70	milk	0.0
protein (gm)	3.0	vegetable	2.0
fat (gm)	2.6	fruit	0.0
cholesterol (mg)	8	bread	0.0
sodium (mg)	116	meat	0.0
% calories from fat	30	fat	0.5

♥

STRING BEAN SALAD

The most common green vegetable in Greece is the string bean, grown in many different varieties. Use fresh beans for this salad because they are infinitely tastier than frozen and well worth the time you spend cutting off the tips.

2 lbs. fresh string beans

½ teaspoon Spike

1 qt. water

1 recipe Italian Dressing (p. 55)

¼ cup onion, chopped

3 tablespoons parsley, minced

Wash beans and trim ends. Add Spike and beans to boiling water, and cook until beans are tender, 8–10 minutes. Drain beans and pour cold water over them to keep them green. Put beans in a bowl, top with Italian dressing, toss well, and refrigerate. About 20 minutes before serving, decorate with onion and parsley.

Serves 6

NUTRITIONAL DATA

PER SERVING		EXCHANGES	
calories	67	milk	0.0
protein (gm)	3.0	vegetable	2.5
fat (gm)	0.5	fruit	0.0

cholesterol (mg)	0	bread	0.0
sodium (mg)	6	meat	0.0
% calories from fat	5	fat	0.0

YOGURT DRESSING

1 cup plain, non-fat yogurt

¼ cup golden raisins

2 tablespoons orange peel, grated

2 tablespoons honey

Combine all ingredients and chill well. Serve cold.
Makes about 1½ cups.
Serves 24 (1 tablespoon per serving)

NUTRITIONAL DATA

PER SERVING		EXCHANGES	
calories	15	milk	0.0
protein (gm)	0.6	vegetable	0.0
fat (gm)	0.0	fruit	0.0
cholesterol (mg)	0	bread	0.0
sodium (mg)	7	meat	0.0
% calories from fat	1	fat	0.0

SPANISH SALADS & DRESSINGS

LISBON SALAD

1 lb. white asparagus

1 lb. string beans

4 plump tomatoes, sliced

½ lb. button mushrooms, sliced

1 bag spinach, washed and dried

16 artichoke hearts

4 carrots, cut into strips

1 cup watercress

2 stalks celery, cut up

2 cucumbers, sliced

1 recipe Italian Dressing (p. 55)

Place a steamer basket in large stockpot and steam asparagus 8–10 minutes. Lift out basket and place asparagus on a plate. Add string beans and steam 6–8 minutes. Lift out basket and place string beans on plate.

On a large platter, artfully arrange asparagus and string beans in center and place remaining vegetables in a pattern of your choosing. Pour Italian dressing over all.

Serves 8

NUTRITIONAL DATA

PER SERVING		EXCHANGES	
calories	95	milk	0.0
protein (gm)	5.6	vegetable	4.0
fat (gm)	0.9	fruit	0.0
cholesterol (mg)	0	bread	0.0
sodium (mg)	94	meat	0.0
% calories from fat	7	fat	0.0

♥

TOMATO AND CUCUMBER SALAD WITH FRESH BASIL

2 heads red leaf lettuce, torn into bite-size pieces

4 large tomatoes, cut into wedges

3 cucumbers, sliced but not peeled

½ cup scallions, cut into 1-in. pieces

⅓ cup mushrooms, sliced

6 large fresh basil leaves, snipped

1 recipe Vinaigrette Dressing (p. 50)

Combine lettuce, tomatoes, cucumbers, scallions, mushrooms, and basil in large bowl. Toss with dressing.

Serves 8

NUTRITIONAL DATA

PER SERVING		EXCHANGES	
calories	36	milk	0.0
protein (gm)	1.8	vegetable	1.5
fat (gm)	0.6	fruit	0.0
cholesterol (mg)	0	bread	0.0
sodium (mg)	11	meat	0.0
% calories from fat	12	fat	0.0

BALSAMIC DRESSING

If you don't have balsamic vinegar, substitute another kind; but if you choose another vinegar, combine water in equal proportions.

¾ cup water

¼ cup balsamic vinegar

3 teaspoons capers

2 teaspoons Dijon mustard

1 teaspoon tarragon

1 teaspoon thyme

1 teaspoon purple basil

1 tablespoon fresh parsley, chopped

Combine all ingredients. Adjust vinegar to taste; you may feel that it has a strong flavor. Store in a covered container.

Makes about 1 cup.

Serves 16 (1 tablespoon per serving)

NUTRITIONAL DATA

PER SERVING		EXCHANGES	
calories	1	milk	0.0
protein (gm)	0.0	vegetable	0.0
fat (gm)	0.0	fruit	0.0
cholesterol (mg)	0	bread	0.0
sodium (mg)	9	meat	0.0
% calories from fat	1	fat	0.0

♥

TOMATO VINAIGRETTE

1 14½-oz. can chunky tomatoes

2 tablespoons white wine vinegar

¼ cup white wine

1 teaspoon basil

½ teaspoon thyme

½ teaspoon Dijon mustard

Combine all ingredients in blender or food processor. Process until smooth. Store in refrigerator about 2 days. Shake well before using.

Makes 1 cup.

Serves 16 (1 tablespoon per serving)

NUTRITIONAL DATA

PER SERVING		EXCHANGES	
calories	8	milk	0.0
protein (gm)	0.2	vegetable	0.0
fat (gm)	0.1	fruit	0.0
cholesterol (mg)	0	bread	0.0
sodium (mg)	42	meat	0.0
% calories from fat	7	fat	0.0

MOROCCAN SALADS

☆

MOROCCAN CARROT SALAD

8 medium carrots

2 teaspoons paprika

½ teaspoon cinnamon

1 teaspoon ground cumin

1 tablespoon fresh lemon juice

1 tablespoon sugar

2 tablespoons white wine

½ teaspoon black pepper, freshly ground

Spike

2 onions, chopped and sauted, kept warm

Peel carrots and thinly slice or cut into julienne strips. You should have about 2 cups.

Place spices, lemon juice, and sugar in mortar and grind with pestle to emulsify. Gradually work in wine. Season to taste with pepper and Spike.

Heat a medium pot of water to boiling. Drop in carrots and cook till tender, about 20 minutes. Drain carrots and put them in a bowl.

Toss immediately with the vinaigrette from the mortar. If carrots seem gritty, add a tablespoon of cold water to smooth out dressing. Add onions and toss again.

Serves 8

NUTRITIONAL DATA

PER SERVING		EXCHANGES	
calories	54	milk	0.0
protein (gm)	1.2	vegetable	2.0
fat (gm)	0.2	fruit	0.0
cholesterol (mg)	0	bread	0.0
sodium (mg)	27	meat	0.0
% calories from fat	3	fat	0.0

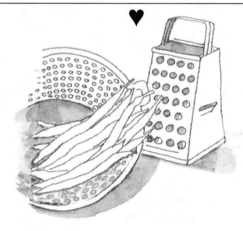

POULTRY

FRENCH POULTRY

■

CHICKEN DIJON

D*ijon is the capital of Burgundy and is known for its famed "Dijon mustard," so it is no surprise to find a recipe from there using wine and mustard.*

1 2½–3 lb. broiler, skinned and quartered
  Vegetable cooking spray (olive-oil flavored)
2 cups white wine
½ teaspoon dried tarragon leaves
  Thyme, pinch
1 bay leaf, small
1 teaspoon Spike
¼ teaspoon pepper
2 tablespoons mustard (Dijon style)
2 tablespoons yogurt, plain low-fat
  Cayenne pepper, pinch

In skillet sprayed with vegetable cooking spray, add chicken and cook until well browned on both sides. Add wine, tarragon, thyme, bay leaf, Spike, and pepper. Bring to boil. Cover and simmer 45 minutes or until meat is tender.

Remove meat to heated serving dish and keep warm. Discard bay leaf.

Blend sauce with mustard, yogurt, and cayenne pepper. Heat, stirring briskly and constantly. Do not allow to boil. Pour over chicken.

Serves 4

NUTRITIONAL DATA

PER SERVING		EXCHANGES	
calories	314	milk	0.0
protein (gm)	42.8	vegetable	0.0
fat (gm)	5.4	fruit	0.0
cholesterol (mg)	115	bread	0.0
sodium (mg)	212	meat	5.0
% calories from fat	16	fat	1.0

COQ-AU-VIN
(Chicken in Red Wine)

1 3½-lb. chicken, skinned

Vegetable cooking spray (olive-oil flavored)

8 small onions or shallots

3 tablespoons brandy

1¼ cups red wine

1¼ cups chicken stock

Black pepper, freshly ground

Bouquet garni (see p. 145)

2 cloves garlic, minced

1 cup mushrooms, sliced

¼ cup all-purpose flour

2 tablespoons parsley, chopped

¼ cup croutons for garnish (optional)

Cut chicken into 4 portions. Spray skillet with vegetable cooking spray and saute chicken until golden; remove and drain. Peel onions and add to skillet. Saute until golden, stirring occasionally.

Return chicken to skillet, pour in brandy and ignite. When flames have died down, add wine, chicken stock, freshly ground pepper, bouquet garni, garlic, and mushrooms. Bring to boil. Cover and simmer gently 35–45 minutes or until chicken is tender. Remove and discard bouquet garni. Remove chicken from skillet and place on heated serving plate.

Add flour to skillet and blend with cooking juices, stirring constantly. Allow gravy to boil 2–3 minutes. Pour gravy over chicken, sprinkle with chopped parsley, and arrange croutons around edge of plate. Serve very hot.

Serves 4

NUTRITIONAL DATA

PER SERVING		EXCHANGES	
calories	450	milk	0.0
protein (gm)	62.1	vegetable	1.0
fat (gm)	7.3	fruit	0.0
cholesterol (mg)	161	bread	0.5
sodium (mg)	391	meat	7.0
% calories from fat	15	fat	0.0

CHICKEN WITH APPLES AND CIDER

1 3½-lb. chicken, skinned
  Vegetable cooking spray (olive-oil flavored)
6 firm apples
  Pepper, freshly ground
3 tablespoons all-purpose flour

2 cups hard cider (divided)

Bouquet garni (see p. 145)

¾ cup evaporated skim milk

2 tablespoons parsley, chopped

Cut chicken into 4 portions. Spray a flameproof casserole with vegetable cooking spray and add chicken. Brown on all sides. Remove and drain.

Peel, core, and slice 2 of the apples, sprinkle with pepper, and saute until beginning to brown. Sprinkle in flour and cook gently, stirring occasionally, until flour is light brown. Add 1¼ cups cider and bring to boil, stirring constantly.

Replace chicken pieces and add bouquet garni. Cover with tightly fitting lid. Cook in moderately hot oven 375°, for 1 hour.

Meanwhile, peel, core, and cut into quarters the remaining 4 apples. Spray a small skillet with vegetable cooking spray and add apples. Saute until browned lightly. Place in ovenproof dish with 3 tablespoons water. Cover and place in oven, under casserole, until needed.

When chicken is cooked, remove it from casserole and place it on heated serving dish. Bring sauce to the boil, add remaining cider, and boil rapidly 10 minutes. Strain and return to rinsed saucepan.

Add apples and milk. Reheat very gently without boiling. Adjust seasoning. Pour over chicken. Garnish with parsley.

Serves 4

NUTRITIONAL DATA

PER SERVING		EXCHANGES	
calories	539	milk	0.5
protein (gm)	63.0	vegetable	0.0
fat (gm)	7.6	fruit	2.0
cholesterol (mg)	162	bread	0.0
sodium (mg)	195	meat	7.0
% calories from fat	13	fat	0.0

■

CHICKEN MARENGO

At the battle of Marengo in 1800, so the story goes, Napoleon's chef was unable to obtain butter for dinner. Using what he had at hand, he sauteed his chicken in olive oil. Napoleon was delighted, and so have been the French ever since. Veal can also be used in this recipe.

1 frying chicken, 2–3 lbs., skinned

⅓ cup flour

1 teaspoon Spike

½ teaspoon black pepper, freshly ground

   Vegetable cooking spray (olive-oil flavored)

1 clove garlic, minced

3 tablespoons onion, chopped

4 tomatoes, quartered

1 cup white wine

   Bouquet garni (see p. 145)

   Vegetable cooking spray (olive-oil flavored)

1 cup mushrooms, sliced

6 large black olives, sliced

½ cup consommé, cold, canned

2 tablespoons flour

2 tablespoons parsley, chopped

Disjoint chicken and cut into serving-size pieces. Rinse and pat dry with absorbent paper. To coat chicken evenly, shake 2 or 3 pieces at a time in plastic bag containing mixture of flour, Spike, and pepper.

Spray skillet with vegetable cooking spray and brown chicken. Add garlic, onion, tomatoes, wine, and bouquet garni. Cover and simmer over low heat about ½ hour, until thickest pieces of chicken are tender when pierced with fork.

In a small skillet sprayed with vegetable cooking spray, saute mushrooms. Add to chicken with olives.

Put consommé and flour into screw-top jar and cover. Shake well. Remove chicken from skillet and discard bouquet garni. Gradually add consommé-flour liquid to mixture in skillet, stirring constantly. Boil 3–5 minutes until mixture thickens. Return chicken to sauce, cover, and simmer 10 minutes.

Arrange chicken on hot platter. Cover with sauce.

Serves 5

NUTRITIONAL DATA

PER SERVING		EXCHANGES	
calories	278	milk	0.0
protein (gm)	30.0	vegetable	1.0
fat (gm)	7.4	fruit	0.0
cholesterol (mg)	73	bread	0.5
sodium (mg)	170	meat	3.0
% calories from fat	24	fat	1.0

ITALIAN POULTRY

■

CHICKEN CACCIATORE

This recipe is wonderful because it can be pre-
pared in advance, it can be doubled, and it
looks great on a buffet.

½ cup flour

2 teaspoons Spike

½ teaspoon pepper

1 3½-lb. broiler-fryer chicken, skinned and cut up
  Vegetable cooking spray (olive-oil flavored)

¼ cup onion, finely chopped

1 clove garlic, minced

1 15½-oz. can low-sodium tomatoes (chunky)

1 small can low-sodium tomato paste

½ cup white wine

1 cup mushrooms, sliced

1 teaspoon oregano

1 teaspoon dried basil

1 bay leaf

¼ cup dry sherry

1 teaspoon sugar

Mix flour, Spike, and pepper together and pour into paper bag.
Wash and pat chicken pieces dry. Put chicken into bag, a few pieces
at a time, and shake to coat evenly.

Heat skillet and spray with vegetable cooking spray; brown chicken pieces on all sides. Remove chicken, add onion and garlic, and cook over moderately low heat about 5 minutes until tender.

Return chicken to skillet; add tomatoes, tomato paste, wine, mushrooms, oregano, basil, and bay leaf. Cover and simmer over moderately low heat 1 hour, stirring occasionally. Stir in sherry and sugar. Cook 15 minutes longer or until fork-tender.

Serves 6

NUTRITIONAL DATA

PER SERVING		EXCHANGES	
calories	332	milk	0.0
protein (gm)	42.2	vegetable	3.0
fat (gm)	5.1	fruit	0.0
cholesterol (mg)	107	bread	0.5
sodium (mg)	123	meat	4.0
% calories from fat	14	fat	0.0

♥

CHICKEN SALTIMBOCCA

3 large chicken breasts, skinned, boned, and halved lengthwise

6 thin slices boiled ham

3 tablespoons part-skim mozzarella cheese, shredded

1 medium tomato, seeded and chopped

1 teaspoon oregano

⅓ cup dry breadcrumbs

2 tablespoons parsley, snipped

Place chicken, boned side up, on cutting board. Place clear plastic wrap over it. Working from the center out, pound lightly with meat mallet to about 5 x 5 in. Remove wrap.

Place ham slice and ½ tablespoon mozzarella cheese on each cutlet. Top with some tomato and dash of oregano. Sprinkle with mixture of breadcrumbs and parsley. Bake in 350° oven 40–45 minutes.

Serves 6

NUTRITIONAL DATA

PER SERVING		EXCHANGES	
calories	204	milk	0.0
protein (gm)	31.0	vegetable	0.5
fat (gm)	5.7	fruit	0.0
cholesterol (mg)	81	bread	0.0
sodium (mg)	172	meat	3.5
% calories from fat	26	fat	0.0

CHICKEN PICCATA

1½ lbs. boneless chicken breasts, split and skinned
Vegetable cooking spray (olive-oil flavored)
½ teaspoon Spike
½ teaspoon tarragon
¼ teaspoon pepper, freshly ground
¼ cup lemon juice
¼ cup butter buds
1 tablespoon capers

On a board, place chicken breasts smooth side down and cover with plastic wrap. Pound each to ¼-in. thickness with mallet. Dry meat with paper towels.

Spray a medium-size skillet with vegetable spray and add a few pieces of chicken. Cook about 4 minutes on each side until golden. Remove to a platter and keep warm while cooking remaining chicken. Sprinkle cooked chicken with Spike, tarragon, and pepper.

Add lemon juice, butter buds, and capers to skillet and cook over moderate heat, stirring to incorporate brown particles from pan. When sauce has reduced, about 5 minutes, return chicken to skillet and continue cooking 5 more minutes.

Serves 6

NUTRITIONAL DATA

PER SERVING		EXCHANGES	
calories	95	milk	0.0
protein (gm)	16.8	vegetable	0.0
fat (gm)	1.9	fruit	0.0
cholesterol (mg)	45	bread	0.0
sodium (mg)	39	meat	2.0
% calories from fat	19	fat	0.0

♥

GREEK POULTRY

The Greeks are very fond of chicken and prepare it in many ways. They have one important step that most Greek cooks insist on prior to cooking chicken in any recipe. That step is to pour boiling water over the chicken to plump and whiten it; then they rub it with half a lemon.

KAPAMA
(Chicken with Spices)

This is a wonderful chicken recipe to serve with pasta or rice.

2 teaspoons Spike
¼ teaspoon black pepper
½ teaspoon ground cloves
½ teaspoon ground cinnamon
2½ tablespoons lemon juice
3 whole broiler or fryer chicken breasts, halved, skinned, and boned
Vegetable cooking spray (olive-oil flavored)
1 large onion, finely chopped
1 clove garlic, minced
¾ cup boiling water
½ cup white wine
6 oz. tomato paste
1 15½-oz. can chunky tomatoes
1 teaspoon sugar

1 tablespoon cornstarch, diluted in ¼ cup cold water (optional)

1 lb. pasta, or 3 cups rice, cooked

3 tablespoons Parmesan or Romano cheese, freshly grated

Combine Spike, pepper, cloves, cinnamon, and lemon juice in mixing bowl. Stir several times with fork. Dip chicken breasts into bowl, coating each piece with marinade.

Spray a 3-qt. pot with vegetable cooking spray and, over low heat, saute half the chicken breasts until golden on both sides, no longer than 8 minutes. Remove them to large plate. Saute other half of the breasts and remove them to the plate.

Using same pot, saute onion and garlic for a few seconds; then add water, wine, tomato paste, canned tomatoes, and sugar. Mix and turn until sauce boils. Cover pot, lower heat, and simmer sauce 1 hour. If you wish sauce thickened, stir in cornstarch mixture after sauce has simmered 40 minutes.

Return chicken to pot and simmer an additional 15 minutes. Serve over pasta or rice, topped with grated cheese.

Serves 6

NUTRITIONAL DATA

PER SERVING		EXCHANGES	
calories	494	milk	0.0
protein (gm)	41.7	vegetable	2.0
fat (gm)	7.3	fruit	0.0
cholesterol (mg)	146	bread	3.0
sodium (mg)	373	meat	4.0
% calories from fat	13	fat	0.0

♥

CLASSIC ROAST CHICKEN WITH LEMON AND HERBS

This chicken dish is an excellent foil for a special potato or vegetable dish because it is so basic and delicious. Make it anytime.

> 1 medium-size roasting chicken (3–4 lbs.)
>
> 3 tablespoons white wine
>
> Spike and freshly ground pepper, to taste
>
> Juice of 2 fresh lemons (about 4 tablespoons)
>
> 2 teaspoons dried thyme
>
> ½ teaspoon crushed rosemary
>
> 1 teaspoon oregano
>
> 2 garlic cloves, minced
>
> 6–8 medium potatoes, quartered lengthwise
>
> 1 cup water

Preheat oven to 450°. In a bowl, combine wine, Spike, pepper, lemon juice, herbs, and garlic. Brush chicken with marinade. Place chicken in medium to large square, shallow pan. Spread potatoes around pan evenly. Pour marinade and 1 cup water over potatoes. Season potatoes with Spike and pepper.

Place pan in hot oven and reduce heat to 350°. Bake 1–1½ hours, basting chicken with pan juices every 10 minutes, until meat is tender. Add water to potatoes during cooking if necessary. Remove chicken from oven as soon as it's tender.

Check potatoes to see if they are done. If not done, turn up oven to 450°, add more water if necessary, and roast another 10 to 15 minutes or until potatoes are golden brown and tender. Serve warm.

Serves 4

NUTRITIONAL DATA

PER SERVING		EXCHANGES	
calories	451	milk	0.0
protein (gm)	54.0	vegetable	0.0
fat (gm)	6.0	fruit	0.0
cholesterol (mg)	137	bread	2.0
sodium (mg)	127	meat	6.0
% calories from fat	12	fat	0.0

SPANISH POULTRY

CHICKEN CATALAN STYLE

1 3-lb. chicken, skinned and cut into serving pieces
Vegetable cooking spray (olive-oil flavored)
½ teaspoon Spike
    Black pepper, freshly ground
2 onions, finely chopped
1 clove garlic, minced
2 tomatoes, peeled, seeded, and chopped
1 bay leaf
½ cup dry white wine
1 small eggplant
1 teaspoon Spike
½ cup water
2 zucchini, sliced
2 green or red bell peppers
½ cup tomato sauce
1 teaspoon cilantro
1 teaspoon basil
2 tablespoons parsley, chopped

Brown chicken in skillet sprayed with vegetable cooking spray. Remove chicken and season with Spike and pepper. Place chicken in casserole.

Saute onions and garlic in same skillet 3 minutes. Add tomatoes, bay leaf, and white wine. Simmer mixture 5 minutes. Transfer to casserole. Cover and cook in preheated 350° oven 30 minutes.

In the meantime, cut eggplant into small cubes and sprinkle with Spike. Allow eggplant to stand 10 minutes to drain bitter juices. Add ½ cup water to skillet and add eggplant and zucchini. Saute over moderate heat 5 minutes until lightly browned.

Remove membranes and seeds from peppers and chop. Add peppers to skillet and saute 5 minutes.

Add eggplant, zucchini, and peppers to casserole. Add tomato sauce, cilantro, and basil. Continue cooking 30 minutes until chicken is tender. Sauce should be thick. Remove bay leaf.

Arrange chicken pieces and sauce on hot serving dish. Top with parsley.

Serves 4

NUTRITIONAL DATA

PER SERVING		EXCHANGES	
calories	402	milk	0.0
protein (gm)	57.2	vegetable	3.0
fat (gm)	8.2	fruit	0.0
cholesterol (mg)	147	bread	0.0
sodium (mg)	327	meat	6.0
% calories from fat	19	fat	0.0

♥

ARROZ CON POLLO
(Chicken with Rice)

Frying chicken, large size, skinned and cut up

Spike

Pepper, freshly ground

Vegetable cooking spray

½ cup onion, chopped

2 cloves garlic, minced

1 medium-size bell pepper (red, green, or yellow), chopped

1 28-oz. can tomatoes (salt free)

2 chicken bouillon cubes (salt free)

1½ cups water

1¼ cups rice, uncooked

1 bay leaf

1 teaspoon paprika

¼ teaspoon saffron

½ teaspoon oregano

1½ teaspoons Spike

1 10-oz. package frozen peas, thawed

2 pimientos, cut into strips

Heat oven to 350°.

Wash and dry chicken. Sprinkle lightly with Spike and pepper. Heat skillet over moderately high heat and spray with vegetable cooking spray. Cook chicken until lightly browned on all sides. Remove chicken and place in deep 3½-qt. casserole or Dutch oven.

Add onion, garlic, and bell pepper to skillet, and cook until tender over moderate heat. Add tomatoes, bouillon cubes, and water; cook and stir about 5 minutes longer. Remove from skillet and mix in rice, bay leaf, paprika, saffron, oregano, and Spike. Pour over chicken.

Cover and bake 25 minutes. Stir in peas. Bake, covered, 15 minutes longer or until rice and chicken are tender. At end of baking time, stir rice. Garnish with strips of pimiento.

Serves 6

NUTRITIONAL DATA

PER SERVING		EXCHANGES	
calories	549	milk	0.0
protein (gm)	56.4	vegetable	2.0
fat (gm)	14.0	fruit	0.0
cholesterol (mg)	140	bread	2.0
sodium (mg)	155	meat	6.5
% calories from fat	23	fat	0.0

♥

MOROCCAN POULTRY

☆

MOROCCAN CHICKEN AND CHICKPEAS

T his dish is great for entertaining because it serves 8 and can be doubled easily.

2 cups (1 lb.) dried chickpeas

2 qts. cold water

3½ teaspoons Spike (divided)

1 onion, peeled and quartered

1 bay leaf

4-lb. ready-to-cook roasting chicken, skinned

2 cloves garlic, crushed

1 teaspoon ground ginger

¼ teaspoon pepper, freshly ground

1 tablespoon water

½ cup onion, chopped

1 teaspoon turmeric

2 tablespoons parsley, chopped

1 (2-in.) cinnamon stick

1 10¾-oz. can condensed chicken broth, undiluted

1 cup onion, sliced

½ cup raisins

The day before you plan to make this meal, pick over chickpeas and place them in large bowl; cover with cold water; refrigerate, covered, overnight.

The next day, drain chickpeas; turn into large pot. Add 2 qts. cold water, 2 teaspoons Spike, quartered onion, and bay leaf. Bring to boil; reduce heat and simmer, covered, 1½ hours or until tender. Drain and set aside. Remove and discard onion and bay leaf.

Meanwhile, rinse chicken well; dry with paper towels. Sprinkle inside with 1 teaspoon Spike. Tuck wings under body; then tie legs together at ends with twine.

In a small bowl, combine garlic, ginger, ½ teaspoon Spike, pepper, and 1 tablespoon water; mix well. Brush mixture over entire surface of chicken. Refrigerate chicken in large bowl, covered with plastic wrap or foil, 1 hour.

In 6-qt. Dutch oven, combine chopped onion, turmeric, chopped parsley, cinnamon stick, and chicken broth. Over medium heat, bring to boil, stirring constantly. Lower heat, then add chicken, breast side down, and any juices left in bottom of bowl. Simmer, covered, 1 hour or until chicken is tender. Turn chicken frequently, using wooden spoons. Remove cooked chicken to serving platter. Discard cinnamon stick.

To sauce left in Dutch oven, add sliced onion, raisins, and drained chickpeas. Bring to boil; cook, stirring frequently, until onion is soft and flavors have blended, about 15 minutes.

Before serving, remove twine. Reheat chicken in chickpea mixture 5 minutes. Serve chicken and chickpeas together.

Serves 8

NUTRITIONAL DATA

PER SERVING		EXCHANGES	
calories	486	milk	0.0
protein (gm)	44.2	vegetable	0.0
fat (gm)	15.5	fruit	0.5
cholesterol (mg)	94	bread	2.0
sodium (mg)	308	meat	5.0
% calories from fat	29	fat	0.5

☆

MOROCCAN STYLE ROAST CHICKEN STUFFED WITH COUSCOUS

STUFFING

¾ cup raisins

3 tablespoons dry white wine

½ teaspoon saffron threads, chopped

1 cup instant couscous

1½ cups water

2 tablespoons olive oil

2 medium onions, chopped

2 teaspoons cinnamon

1 tablespoon honey

Spike and freshly ground pepper

BASTING BUTTER

1 cup butter buds

¼ cup dark honey

¾ teaspoon cinnamon

¼ teaspoon turmeric, or ground cumin

Spike and freshly ground pepper

4 Rock Cornish game hens, about 1½ lbs. each, skinned

Stuffing: Soak raisins in hot water to cover for 30 minutes; drain and set aside.

Heat wine in small saucepan over medium heat until warm. Remove from heat, add saffron, and let steep 15 minutes.

Put couscous in shallow baking dish (9-in. square will do nicely). In saucepan, heat water until boiling, then pour over couscous and stir well. Cover with foil and let stand 15 minutes. Fluff couscous with fork.

Add olive oil to medium saute pan over medium heat. Add chopped onions, and cook until tender and translucent, 8–10 minutes. Add cinnamon and cook 2 minutes. Add saffron-infused wine and cook 1 minute.

Stir onion mixture, raisins, and honey into couscous. Season to taste with Spike and pepper. Let cool.

Basting Butter: To butter buds, add honey, cinnamon, and turmeric. Season to taste with Spike and pepper; set aside.

Preheat oven to 450°. Spoon cooled stuffing (above) into cavities of hens. Place hens on rack in shallow roasting or sheet pan. Baste occasionally with the "butter," until juices run clear when thigh is pierced with skewer, about 45 minutes.

Serves 8

NUTRITIONAL DATA

PER SERVING		EXCHANGES	
calories	596	milk	0.0
protein (gm)	51.0	vegetable	0.0
fat (gm)	22.5	fruit	1.0
cholesterol (mg)	140	bread	2.0
sodium (mg)	86	meat	6.0
% calories from fat	35	fat	2.0

MEATS

FRENCH MEATS

██

BOEUF À LA BOURGUIGNONNE
(Beef Burgundy Style)

*T*his *gastronomical masterpiece is typical of a dish designed to play up the wines for which Burgundy is so famous.*

- 1 cup beef bouillon
- 3 tablespoons flour
- 1 tablespoon tomato paste
- 2 lbs. lean beef, round or chuck
  - Vegetable cooking spray (olive-oil flavored)
- 2 tablespoons sherry wine
- 1½ cups onion, chopped
- 1 cup Burgundy, or other red wine
  - Bouquet garni (sprig of parsley with 1 teaspoon each thyme, rosemary, tarragon in cheesecloth bag)
- 12 medium-size mushrooms
- 1 teaspoon *herbes de Provençe*
- 3 tablespoons fresh parsley, chopped

Set out large skillet with tight-fitting cover.

In a mixing bowl, make a paste of bouillon, flour, and tomato paste.

Wipe beef with clean, damp cloth and cut into 3-in. pieces. Spray skillet with vegetable cooking spray and add meat. Brown on all sides. Remove meat from skillet and set aside.

Stir into skillet sherry and onions. Cook onions until transparent, stirring often. Blend in tomato paste mixture. Bring rapidly to boil, stirring constantly. Then stir in red wine and add bouquet garni.

Replace beef. Cover and simmer over low heat 2½–3 hours or until meat is tender.

Meanwhile clean and slice mushrooms. Add to meat with *herbes de Provence*. Cook an additional 15 minutes. Remove and discard bouquet garni. Turn meat into casserole or serving dish. Sprinkle with parsley.

Serves 6

NUTRITIONAL DATA

PER SERVING		EXCHANGES	
calories	277	milk	0.0
protein (gm)	30.0	vegetable	2.0
fat (gm)	9.6	fruit	0.0
cholesterol (mg)	85	bread	0.0
sodium (mg)	234	meat	4.0
% calories from fat	32	fat	0.0

♥

VEAL CHOPS EN PAPILLOTE

Cooking in paper (en papillote) is one of the oldest of French culinary customs. It is used for fish, lamb, and veal chops.

8 thin veal chops

¼ cup white wine

1 teaspoon basil

½ teaspoon oregano

½ teaspoon thyme

8 pieces parchment-type paper

Vegetable cooking spray

½ cup mushrooms, sliced

¼ cup onion, chopped

2 tablespoons fresh parsley, chopped

2 teaspoons black olives, chopped

1 teaspoon Spike

⅛ teaspoon black pepper, freshly ground

Set out a 1-qt. casserole with cover. Wipe veal chops with clean, damp cloth. Put meat into casserole with wine and herbs. Cover and let stand in refrigerator 12 hours to marinate. Turn chops occasionally.

Cut 8 pieces of parchment-type paper large enough to wrap around each chop, allowing margin for overlapping. Lightly spray one side of paper with vegetable cooking spray.

In a small bowl, mix mushrooms, onion, parsley, and olives. Place a heaping tablespoon of mixture on sprayed side of each paper. Place chop on top. Draw paper tightly around each chop, and tie excess paper at top with string so no steam or juice will escape.

Place chops on baking sheet and bake at 300° for 30–40 minutes. Remove papers. Season chops with mixture of Spike and pepper.

Serves 8

NUTRITIONAL DATA

PER SERVING		EXCHANGES	
calories	148	milk	0.0
protein (gm)	22.3	vegetable	0.0
fat (gm)	5.0	fruit	0.0
cholesterol (mg)	93	bread	0.0
sodium (mg)	80	meat	3.0
% calories from fat	32	fat	0.0

♥

■

ROAST SIRLOIN BÉARNAISE

6 lbs. beef, boneless sirloin roast

Garlic powder

Black pepper, freshly ground

Spike

1 recipe Light Béarnaise Sauce (p. 218)

Place roast, fat side up, on rack in shallow roasting pan. Sprinkle generously with garlic powder, pepper, and Spike. Roast in 350° oven 1½–1¾ hours or until thermometer registers 135° (rare). Let stand 5 minutes before carving.

Top with Béarnaise sauce.

Serves 12

NUTRITIONAL DATA

PER SERVING		EXCHANGES	
calories	346	milk	0.0
protein (gm)	45.8	vegetable	0.0
fat (gm)	14.3	fruit	0.0
cholesterol (mg)	129	bread	0.0
sodium (mg)	149	meat	6.0
% calories from fat	38	fat	0.0

♥

■ ▮

RACK OF LAMB À LA PROVENÇAL

This is a classic preparation, where the lamb is covered with a mustard and herb crumb coating so it stays moist during roasting. In the true tradition, serve with Tomato Compote (recipe follows).

ROAST LAMB

Vegetable cooking spray (olive-oil flavored)

½ cup breadcrumbs

1 clove garlic, minced

1 teaspoon shallots, minced

1 rack of lamb (8 ribs, about 2 lbs.)

Spike and freshly ground black pepper

1½ tablespoons Dijon mustard

½ teaspoon fresh oregano, chopped, or pinch dried

½ teaspoon fresh thyme, chopped, or pinch dried

½ teaspoon fresh basil, chopped

1 teaspoon fresh parsley, chopped

TOMATO COMPOTE

1 cup tomatoes, peeled, seeded, and chopped, or 1, 15½-oz. can chunky tomatoes

1 tablespoon fresh basil, chopped

2 tablespoons fresh parsley, chopped

1 tablespoon pitted black olives, coarsely chopped

1½ teaspoons fresh lemon juice

1 clove garlic, minced

½ teaspoon shallots, minced

Spike and freshly ground black pepper

Several sprigs assorted fresh herbs or parsley for garnish

Roast Lamb: Preheat oven to 450°.

Spray a small skillet with vegetable cooking spray and add breadcrumbs, garlic, and shallots. Saute, stirring constantly, about 3 minutes or until just golden. Remove from skillet and set aside.

Using sharp knife, cut chine bone away from lamb rack. Place rack, ribs curved downward, on cutting board. Trim all visible fat from the rack.

Spray a large skillet with vegetable cooking spray and place over medium-high heat. Season lamb with Spike and pepper, and sear it 2–3 minutes on each side.

In a small bowl, combine mustard, oregano, thyme, basil, and parsley. Spread mixture over top of lamb rack, and then cover with the breadcrumb mixture. Place lamb on roasting rack over roasting pan or baking sheet, and roast 25–30 minutes or until meat thermometer registers 140°F. for medium-rare. Let stand 5 minutes before carving into chops.

Tomato Compote: While lamb is roasting, combine all compote ingredients in a bowl and season with Spike and pepper. Let stand at room temperature up to 30 minutes. Arrange chops on plates and then add a dollop of compote. Garnish with sprigs of fresh herbs.

Serves 4

NUTRITIONAL DATA

PER SERVING		EXCHANGES	
calories	317	milk	0.0
protein (gm)	31.6	vegetable	0.0
fat (gm)	16.1	fruit	0.0
cholesterol (mg)	99	bread	0.5
sodium (mg)	261	meat	4.0
% calories from fat	47	fat	1.0

ITALIAN MEATS

▮

VEAL PICCATA

This makes an excellent company dinner. It is particularly good with pasta.

1 lb. veal, thinly sliced

3 tablespoons flour

Vegetable cooking spray (olive-oil flavored)

1½ cups mushrooms, sliced

½ lemon

½ cup dry white wine

3 tablespoons fresh parsley, chopped

8 lemon slices

Cut veal slices into serving pieces, then coat each piece with flour. Spray skillet with vegetable cooking spray and add veal. Cook over high heat until lightly browned on both sides. Add sliced mushrooms and saute until lightly browned. Squeeze lemon over veal in pan; then add wine. Stir all ingredients, and cook 1 minute more. Arrange veal on serving platter, garnishing with parsley and lemon slices.

Serves 4

▬
NUTRITIONAL DATA

PER SERVING		EXCHANGES	
calories	155	milk	0.0
protein (gm)	18.1	vegetable	0.0

fat (gm)	4.0	fruit	0.0
cholesterol (mg)	71	bread	0.5
sodium (mg)	62	meat	2.0
% calories from fat	23	fat	0.0

♥

Note: Linguine with Garlic and Peppers Sauce (p. 225) is wonderful with this type of veal. You can also substitute boned chicken breasts for veal.

VEAL MARSALA WITH MUSHROOMS

1 lb. (1¼-in. thick) veal

Vegetable cooking spray

½ teaspoon dried whole rosemary, crushed

¼ teaspoon Spike

½ teaspoon pepper, freshly ground

1 teaspoon olive oil

2 cloves garlic, minced

2 cups mushrooms, sliced

1 teaspoon cornstarch

⅓ cup chicken broth

⅓ cup dry Marsala wine

Put veal between 2 pieces of wax paper and pound thin. Spray skillet with cooking spray and add veal and seasonings. Saute 2 minutes, then add olive oil and garlic. Saute 2 more minutes, then add mushrooms.

While mushrooms are cooking, mix cornstarch in chicken broth and add to veal mixture along with wine. Cook on low heat about 10 more minutes.

Serves 4

NUTRITIONAL DATA

PER SERVING		EXCHANGES	
calories	134	milk	0.0
protein (gm)	18.1	vegetable	1.0
fat (gm)	4.0	fruit	0.0
cholesterol (mg)	71	bread	0.0
sodium (mg)	126	meat	2.0
% calories from fat	27	fat	0.0

♥

Note: You can substitute chicken for veal. It's much cheaper and very delicious.

PORK CHOPS PARMESAN

3 tablespoons cornmeal, or whole-wheat flour, or breadcrumbs

1 tablespoon Parmesan cheese, grated

½ teaspoon black pepper, freshly ground

½ teaspoon Spike

½ teaspoon basil

4 pork loin rib chops, about ½-in. thick

Vegetable cooking spray (olive-oil flavored)

3 green onions, chopped

1 clove garlic, minced

¼ teaspoon fennel seeds, crushed

3 tablespoons fresh parsley, chopped

Combine cornmeal, Parmesan cheese, black pepper, Spike, and basil. Trim pork chops of all visible fat, pat dry, and dredge in cornmeal mixture.

Spray skillet with vegetable cooking spray and place over medium heat. Place chops in skillet and reduce heat to low. Saute chops 10 minutes on each side. Then add onion, garlic, and fennel; continue sauteing another 10 minutes, stirring to keep from sticking.

Place chops on platter and sprinkle with parsley.
Serves 4

NUTRITIONAL DATA

PER SERVING		EXCHANGES	
calories	174	milk	0.0
protein (gm)	26.3	vegetable	0.0
fat (gm)	4.9	fruit	0.0
cholesterol (mg)	82	bread	0.0
sodium (mg)	91	meat	3.0
% calories from fat	26	fat	0.0

♥

TENDERLOIN FILLETS WITH VEGETABLES AND TWO WINES

Vegetable cooking spray (olive-oil flavored)

⅔ cup celery, sliced

1½ cups red bell pepper, cored, seeded, and cut into strips ¼ in. wide and about 1½ in. long

1½ cups eggplant, peeled and cut into cubes

1 cup romaine lettuce, shredded very fine

1 lb. beef tenderloin, cut into ⅔-in.-thick slices

½ cup dry white wine

½ cup dry Marsala

Spike

Black pepper, freshly ground

Spray a large skillet with vegetable cooking spray. Add celery, bell pepper, and eggplant, and cook vegetables on medium-high setting until they are tender but not mushy. Add shredded lettuce and cook another 2–3 minutes, stirring frequently. Transfer vegetables from skillet to a dish, using slotted spoon.

Add meat to skillet in a single layer, without overlapping it. Brown meat quickly, 1–2 minutes each side, and transfer it to a dish. Add white wine and Marsala to skillet, letting liquid evaporate. Add any additional liquid that might have drained from the fillets in the dish. Scrape bottom of skillet with a wooden spoon to loosen any cooking residues.

When all liquid in skillet, except for the fat, has evaporated, return vegetables and meat. Add Spike and pepper to taste, and cook just long enough to reheat meat and vegetables, no more than 1 minute. Serve at once, pouring all juices from skillet over meat.

Serves 4

NUTRITIONAL DATA

PER SERVING		EXCHANGES	
calories	219	milk	0.0
protein (gm)	22.5	vegetable	2.0
fat (gm)	7.2	fruit	0.0
cholesterol (mg)	64	bread	0.0
sodium (mg)	71	meat	3.0
% calories from fat	30	fat	0.0

♥

SAUTEED VEAL WITH PEPPERS AND OLIVES

1 lb. veal, thinly sliced and lightly pounded

¼ cup flour, for dusting

2 medium-size yellow bell peppers, cored and sliced

1 medium-size red bell pepper, cored and sliced

1 medium-size green bell pepper, cored and sliced

3 cloves garlic, minced

2 teaspoons fresh basil leaves

1 teaspoon fresh rosemary leaves, lightly crushed (omit if only dried are available)

½ teaspoon fresh thyme leaves, or ¼ teaspoon dried thyme, crushed

Vegetable cooking spray (olive-oil flavored)

1½ cups ripe tomatoes, chopped, peeled, and seeded (canned chunky tomatoes may be used)

1 cup beef broth (salt free)

1 cup dry red wine, such as zinfandel

¼ cup Marsala

6 black olives, sliced

Juice of ½ lemon (1 tablespoon)

2 tablespoons chopped fresh basil and parsley combined

Cut veal into serving pieces and lightly dust with flour; set aside.

Saute peppers over high heat with garlic, basil, rosemary, and thyme, using vegetable cooking spray. Remove from skillet. In several batches, quickly saute veal over high heat in same skillet until lightly browned. Remove from pan and set aside with peppers.

Add tomatoes to skillet, along with broth, red wine, and Marsala, and boil to reduce in volume while you stir to blend brown bits left from sauteing. Cook to reduce to about 1 cup.

Return peppers and meat to sauce, toss in olives, and squeeze lemon juice over all. Serve immediately topped with basil and parsley.

Serves 4

NUTRITIONAL DATA

PER SERVING		EXCHANGES	
calories	240	milk	0.0
protein (gm)	20.1	vegetable	1.0
fat (gm)	5.6	fruit	0.0
cholesterol (mg)	72	bread	1.0
sodium (mg)	252	meat	2.5
% calories from fat	21	fat	0.0

♥

GREEK MEATS

DOLMADES
(Stuffed Grape Leaves)

This is a very festive dish and can be placed in a chafing dish on the buffet for quite a long time.

  2 lbs. ground turkey

  ½ lb. ground beef (use ground round if possible)

  2 egg whites

  ½ cup rice

  1 medium onion, finely chopped

  1 teaspoon Spike

  ½ teaspoon pepper, freshly ground

  ½ teaspoon oregano

  ½ teaspoon garlic powder

  1 1-lb. jar grape leaves in brine

  1 46-oz. can tomato juice, low sodium

Mix first 9 ingredients well. Roll 1 rounded teaspoon of meat mixture in each grape leaf. Large leaves may be cut in half. Place so veined, or underside, of leaf is next to meat mixture. Fold leaves; place in large flat pan or skillet. Cover with tomato juice. Simmer 1½ hours. Flavor is improved by reheating. May also be frozen.
  Serves 16

NUTRITIONAL DATA

PER SERVING		EXCHANGES	
calories	159	milk	0.0
protein (gm)	15.0	vegetable	1.0
fat (gm)	7.8	fruit	0.0
cholesterol (mg)	9	bread	0.0
sodium (mg)	110	meat	2.0
% calories from fat	42	fat	0.5

SPANISH MEATS

LOIN OF PORK IN WINE SAUCE

¼ cup white wine

1 clove garlic, minced

5 peppercorns, crushed

4 thick slices pork tenderloin, or 4 pork chops

Vegetable cooking spray

½ cup flour, seasoned with ½ teaspoon Spike and freshly ground black pepper

1 onion, chopped

¼ cup beef broth

¼ cup dry white wine

1 tablespoon dry red wine vinegar

2 tablespoons fresh parsley, chopped

Combine wine, garlic, and peppercorns in bowl. Add pork and turn pieces to coat. Cover with plastic wrap and marinate overnight, turning pork occasionally.

Dry pork with paper towels and dredge in flour mixture. Add pork and marinade to heated skillet sprayed with vegetable cooking spray. Saute on both sides until golden brown. Remove from pan. Add onions to skillet and saute until softened. Add beef broth, wine, and wine vinegar and stir with tidbits left in pan.

Return pork to pan and simmer slowly, uncovered, 30 minutes, turning pork after 15 minutes. If sauce tends to stick, add 1 tablespoon more broth from time to time. Sprinkle with parsley and serve immediately from pan.

Serves 4

NUTRITIONAL DATA

PER SERVING		EXCHANGES	
calories	238	milk	0.0
protein (gm)	27.4	vegetable	0.0
fat (gm)	4.4	fruit	0.0
cholesterol (mg)	81	bread	1.0
sodium (mg)	111	meat	3.0
% calories from fat	17	fat	0.0

MOROCCAN MEATS

PINCHITOS
(Lamb Kabobs with Spicy Lemon Sauce)

SAUCE

½ cup boiling water

3 small, dried, hot red chilies, such as cayenne, tepin, or hontaka, crumbled

2 teaspoons cumin

2 teaspoons paprika

5 cloves garlic, minced

¼ cup lemon juice

2 tablespoons white wine

3 tablespoons cilantro, chopped

½ lemon or lime, peel and all, finely chopped (you can do this in a food processor)

LAMB KABOBS

2½ lbs. lamb shoulder or leg, cut into ½-in.-thick slices

Spike and pepper to taste

1 teaspoon fresh thyme leaves, or ½ teaspoon dried thyme

Vegetable cooking spray

2-3 tomatoes, sliced

Sauce: Pour boiling water over crumbled chilies; let stand until it reaches room temperature. Puree mixture in blender or processor.

Combine cumin, paprika, and garlic with lemon juice. Stir in wine, cilantro, and lemon or lime. Add pureed chilies, and set sauce aside while you prepare meat.

Lamb Kabobs: Sprinkle meat with Spike, pepper, and thyme. Either saute, using vegetable cooking spray, or thread meat onto skewers with tomatoes and grill until medium rare. When halfway cooked, spoon a little sauce onto meat. Serve meat with remaining sauce. Rice or potatoes and salad make good accompaniments.

Serves 6

NUTRITIONAL DATA

PER SERVING		EXCHANGES	
calories	232	milk	0.0
protein (gm)	40	vegetable	0.0
fat (gm)	8.5	fruit	0.0
cholesterol (mg)	95	bread	0.0
sodium (mg)	77	meat	4.0
% calories from fat	37	fat	0.0

♥

SEAFOOD

FRENCH SEAFOOD

■

BAKED COD PROVENÇAL

4 cod fillets, about 1¼ lbs.

Vegetable cooking spray

1 medium-size onion, chopped

2 cloves garlic, finely chopped

1½ lbs. tomatoes, seeded, drained, and chopped

1 tablespoon capers

¼ cup chopped fresh basil or 1 teaspoon dried and crumbled

4 black olives, sliced

1 tablespoon lemon juice

1 teaspoon oregano, crumbled

½ teaspoon Spike

¼ teaspoon pepper, freshly ground

Preheat oven to 450°. Arrange fillets in 8x8x2-in.-square baking dish. Bake 10 minutes or until cooked through.

Spray a medium-size skillet with vegetable cooking spray, and add onion and garlic. Saute over medium heat 3–5 minutes or until onions are translucent. Add tomatoes, capers, basil, olives, lemon juice, oregano, Spike, and pepper. Simmer, stirring occasionally, 8–10 minutes. Spoon sauce over fish.

Serves 4

NUTRITIONAL DATA

PER SERVING		EXCHANGES	
calories	171	milk	0.0
protein (gm)	27.3	vegetable	1.0
fat (gm)	2.2	fruit	0.0
cholesterol (mg)	52	bread	0.0
sodium (mg)	136	meat	3.0
% calories from fat	11	fat	0.0

♥

FRESH SALMON WITH TOMATO SAUCE

Vegetable cooking spray

2 shallots, finely minced

4 medium tomatoes, peeled, cored, seeded, and chopped, or 1 can (15½-oz.) chunky tomatoes

½ cup low-fat yogurt

4 salmon fillets, with skin attached, each about 4 ozs.

Spike

1 large bunch fresh basil

Spray medium-size skillet with vegetable cooking spray. Over medium heat, saute shallots until soft, but not browned, about 2–3 minutes. Add tomatoes and continue cooking until much of the liquid has cooked away, about 10 minutes.

Remove from the heat and when cooled, place in blender. Add yogurt and process until smooth.

Preheat oven to 325°. Place salmon in casserole and spoon sauce over fish. Bake 20 minutes. Sprinkle fish with pinch of Spike and dash of basil, and cook 10 more minutes.

Serves 4

NUTRITIONAL DATA

PER SERVING		EXCHANGES	
calories	149	milk	0.0
protein (gm)	14.1	vegetable	1.0
fat (gm)	6.8	fruit	0.0
cholesterol (mg)	39	bread	0.0
sodium (mg)	58	meat	2.0
% calories from fat	40	fat	0.5

♥

BOUILLABAISSE

This rich and savory stew may be found in every French seaport bordering the Mediterranean, especially in Marseilles, where it originated.

1½ lbs. bass

1 lb. perch

1 lb. fresh shrimp

1 lobster (optional)

   Vegetable cooking spray

⅔ cup onion, chopped

2 leeks (white part only), chopped

3 cloves garlic, minced

4 lbs. very ripe tomatoes, chopped

1 tablespoon parsley, minced

1 bay leaf

½ teaspoon savory

½ teaspoon fennel

⅛ teaspoon saffron

1½ teaspoon Spike

¼ teaspoon pepper

1 pt. oysters

6 slices French bread, toasted

Set out a 3-qt. kettle. Spray with vegetable cooking spray.

Clean, remove bones, and wash fish in cold water. Cut fish into 2-in.-thick pieces. Shell and devein shrimp. Kill and clean lobster and cut into 2-in. pieces. Set seafood aside.

Place onion, leeks, and garlic in sprayed kettle. Cook till onion is translucent, about 10 minutes. Add tomatoes, parsley, bay leaf, savory, fennel, and saffron. Continue cooking about 10 more minutes.

Add lobster and bass, with just enough water to cover. Season with Spike and pepper. Bring rapidly to boil. Simmer 10 minutes. Add perch. Continue to simmer 10 minutes or until fish are almost tender. Add shrimp and cook 5 minutes longer.

Meanwhile, drain oysters, reserving liquid, and pick over to remove shell particles. Simmer in reserved liquid 3 minutes or until edges begin to curl. Add to fish mixture.

Line a deep serving dish with 6 slices toasted French bread. Cover with fish and pour sauce over all. Serve at once.

Serves 8

NUTRITIONAL DATA

PER SERVING		EXCHANGES	
calories	380	milk	0.0
protein (gm)	46.8	vegetable	3.0
fat (gm)	6.7	fruit	0.0
cholesterol (mg)	218	bread	1.0
sodium (mg)	458	meat	4.0
% calories from fat	16	fat	0.0

FILLET OF SOLE VERONIQUE

A great company dish that's quick to make. Serve with chilled white wine and green salad.

1½ lbs. fillet of sole (4 fillets)

   Spike

¾ cup dry white wine

   Vegetable cooking spray

1 tablespoon flour

⅓ cup evaporated skim milk

1 8-oz. can seedless green grapes, drained, or ¾ cup fresh seedless grapes

Sprinkle cold fillets with Spike and place them in a skillet. Pour wine over fish.

Cut a small hole in center of a piece of wax paper exactly the size of skillet. Spray wax paper with vegetable cooking spray and place it, sprayed side down, on top of fish.

Bring liquid in skillet to a boil. Simmer over low heat 10–12 minutes until fish flakes easily when tested with fork. Using a large, broad spatula, remove fish to serving platter. Place in warm oven.

Reserve cooking liquid and place it in a saucepan. Slowly add flour and continue stirring with whisk while mixture cooks. Continue cooking until sauce is thickened and smooth. There should be about 1 cup of sauce.

Add evaporated skim milk to sauce, along with grapes. Heat to just below boiling. Remove from heat, and pour over fish fillets.

Serves 4

NUTRITIONAL DATA

PER SERVING		EXCHANGES	
calories	348	milk	1.5
protein (gm)	43.3	vegetable	0.0
fat (gm)	2.3	fruit	0.5
cholesterol (mg)	87	bread	0.0
sodium (mg)	349	meat	4.0
% calories from fat	6	fat	0.0

▮▮

COQUILLES SAINT JACQUES
(Scallops Baked in Shells)

2 cups dry white wine

Vegetable cooking spray

Bouquet garni (see p. 145)

2 lbs. (1 qt.) scallops

1 teaspoon Spike

½ lb. mushrooms

6 shallots

1 tablespoon parsley, minced

½ cup butter buds (divided)

1 teaspoon lemon juice

¼ cup flour

¼ cup evaporated skim milk, or Mock Crème Fraîche (p. 219)

⅓ cup breadcrumbs

Spray 6 baking shells or ramekins with vegetable cooking spray. Heat in saucepan, wine and bouquet garni.

Wash scallops in cold water and drain. Add scallops, with Spike, to wine. Cover and simmer about 10 minutes or until tender. Remove bouquet garni, drain scallops, and reserve liquid. Cut scallops into bite-size pieces and set aside.

Clean and chop mushrooms and add to a saucepan with shallots, parsley, and ¼ cup butter buds. Add lemon juice and simmer 5–10 minutes. Strain liquid into seasoned wine. Add vegetable mixture to scallops. Set aside.

Make a roux by combining ¼ cup butter buds and flour in a saucepan. Cook over low heat until mixture bubbles. Remove from heat and gradually stir in wine-vegetable liquid. Return to heat and bring rapidly to boil, stirring constantly; cook 1–2 minutes longer.

Remove sauce from heat and gradually add skim milk, or mock crème fraîche, stirring vigorously. Add to scallop mixture.

Fill shells or ramekins, piling high in center. Sprinkle with breadcrumbs. Place in oven at 450° for 8–10 minutes to brown and serve.

Serves 6

NUTRITIONAL DATA

PER SERVING		EXCHANGES	
calories	256	milk	0.0
protein (gm)	28.6	vegetable	0.5
fat (gm)	1.7	fruit	0.0
cholesterol (mg)	50	bread	0.5
sodium (mg)	304	meat	4.0
% calories from fat	6	fat	0.0

ITALIAN SEAFOOD

SCAMPI

1 cup butter buds
¼ cup lemon juice
  Pepper to taste
3 tablespoons shallots, finely minced
4 garlic cloves, finely minced
2 lbs. jumbo shrimp or prawns, shelled and deveined
1 cup mushrooms, sliced
  Lemon slices for garnish
3 tablespoons chopped parsley for garnish

Combine butter buds, lemon juice, pepper, and shallots with garlic in shallow baking dish. Add shrimp, turning several times to coat thoroughly. Add mushrooms and mix well.

Place dish of shrimp in preheated broiler about 4 in. from heat; broil about 2 minutes, turn, and broil on other side 1 minute. Don't overcook.

Arrange on serving platter and pour remaining sauce over shrimp. Garnish with lemon and parsley.

Serves 8

NUTRITIONAL DATA

PER SERVING		EXCHANGES	
calories	105	milk	0.0
protein (gm)	19.0	vegetable	0.0
fat (gm)	1.0	fruit	0.0

cholesterol (mg)	174	bread	0.0
sodium (mg)	201	meat	2.0
% calories from fat	10	fat	0.0

♥

BAKED SHRIMP WITH ASPARAGUS

2 lbs. asparagus

2 lbs. medium shrimp, in shells

½ lb. potatoes

   Vegetable cooking spray

⅔ cup onion, chopped

¼ cup evaporated skim milk

¼ cup Parmesan cheese, freshly grated

1 teaspoon basil

¼ cup seasoned breadcrumbs

Trim asparagus, cutting off 1 in. of hard root from lower half of stalk. Wash thoroughly in 1 or 2 changes of cold water. Place asparagus in steamer basket over boiling water and steam till barely tender, about 8 minutes. Drain and set aside to cool. When asparagus has cooled, cut into pieces 1½ in. long.

Shell shrimp and devein. Wash in cold water. Pat thoroughly dry with paper towels. Set aside.

Wash potatoes and boil them, unpeeled, in large pot of water. When done, drain, peel, and pass potatoes through a food mill or potato ricer into bowl large enough to accommodate all other ingredients.

Spray a medium saucepan with vegetable cooking spray and add onion. Over medium heat, saute onion until it becomes translucent. Add asparagus, turn up heat to high, and saute asparagus, turning it constantly, 3–4 minutes.

Transfer asparagus with all pan juices to bowl containing potatoes. Add milk and cheese. Mix well. Add basil and shrimp and toss to mix well.

Choose a large oven-to-table baking dish. Spray bottom with vegetable spray. Pour into it entire contents of bowl, leveling with a large spoon, and sprinkle on breadcrumbs. Bake on top level of preheated oven 15–20 minutes at 450°.

Serves 8

NUTRITIONAL DATA

PER SERVING		EXCHANGES	
calories	201	milk	0.0
protein (gm)	23.8	vegetable	1.0
fat (gm)	5.8	fruit	0.0
cholesterol (mg)	177	bread	0.5
sodium (mg)	295	meat	2.0
% calories from fat	26	fat	1.0

ITALIAN FISH STEW

1 tablespoon olive oil

3 large garlic cloves, minced

1½ lbs. fresh or canned tomatoes (with juice), peeled and chopped

1 tablespoon oregano

1 teaspoon thyme

1 small bunch parsley, chopped

¼ teaspoon hot pepper flakes to taste

½ cup dry white wine

½ cup mushrooms, sliced

4 large (about 6 ozs. each), thinly cut grouper steaks, or other firm-fleshed fish

Spike to taste

Black pepper, freshly ground

Heat olive oil in large casserole and saute garlic over medium-low heat until golden. Add tomatoes, herbs, parsley, and hot pepper flakes. Bring to simmer and cook, stirring, 10 minutes. Add white wine and mushrooms and bring back to simmer. Add fish and cook 10 more minutes until fish are cooked through. Season to taste with Spike and pepper. To serve, place a fish steak on each plate and spoon sauce over.

Serves 4

NUTRITIONAL DATA

PER SERVING		EXCHANGES	
calories	247	milk	0.0
protein (gm)	34.7	vegetable	1.5
fat (gm)	5.7	fruit	0.0
cholesterol (mg)	62	bread	0.0
sodium (mg)	88	meat	4.0
% calories from fat	21	fat	0.0

GREEK SEAFOOD

SHRIMP WITH FETA CHEESE

Vegetable cooking spray

4 scallions, finely chopped, including green part

2 green peppers, finely chopped

1 small red chili pepper, finely chopped

1 bunch parsley, finely chopped

1 teaspoon oregano

Black pepper, fresh ground, to taste

½ lb. medium-size shrimp, washed, peeled, and deveined

4 medium-size tomatoes, peeled and chopped

1 teaspoon sugar

¼ cup feta cheese, crumbled

3-4 tablespoons skim milk

Spray large skillet with vegetable cooking spray and add scallions. Saute until translucent. Add green peppers, chili pepper, parsley, oregano, and black pepper. Continue sauteing another 5 minutes.

Reduce heat, add shrimp, and cook, uncovered, at least 4 minutes, stirring occasionally with wooden spoon. Add tomatoes and sugar, and simmer another 5 minutes. Finally, add cheese and milk to skillet and simmer, uncovered, over low heat for an additional 20 minutes.

Serves 4

NUTRITIONAL DATA

PER SERVING		EXCHANGES	
calories	130	milk	0.0
protein (gm)	13.4	vegetable	1.0
fat (gm)	4.1	fruit	0.0
cholesterol (mg)	100	bread	0.0
sodium (mg)	279	meat	1.5
% calories from fat	27	fat	0.5

SPANISH SEAFOOD

FISH BASQUE

Vegetable cooking spray

1-1½ lbs. fish fillets (or steaks): sole, grouper, orange roughy, cod, swordfish, salmon, or flounder

¼ cup bottled clam juice

½ cup dry white wine

½ cup canned tomatoes, drained and mashed

2 tablespoons parsley, chopped

½ teaspoon Spike

3 tablespoons scallions, chopped

1 teaspoon thyme

1 bay leaf

Black pepper, freshly ground

Spray a 10-in. skillet with vegetable cooking spray. Lay fish in skillet. Add clam juice, wine, tomatoes, parsley, scallions, Spike, thyme, and bay leaf. Cover. Cook over medium heat 15 minutes. Discard bay leaf.

Remove fish to heated serving dish and keep warm. Raise heat under skillet and cook, without allowing to boil, until liquid is reduced to approximately 3 tablespoons. Add pepper and pour sauce over fish. Serve hot.

Serves 4

NUTRITIONAL DATA

PER SERVING		EXCHANGES	
calories	126	milk	0.0
protein (gm)	19.3	vegetable	0.5
fat (gm)	1.3	fruit	0.0
cholesterol (mg)	53	bread	0.0
sodium (mg)	194	meat	2.0
% calories from fat	10	fat	0.0

♥

COD WITH GREEN SAUCE

1½ lbs. fresh asparagus

2 tablespoons olive oil

2 cloves garlic, crushed

1 tablespoon parsley, chopped

2 lbs. cod, cut into 4 slices

1 tablespoon lemon juice

½ teaspoon Spike

Black pepper, freshly ground

Cut off woody ends of asparagus and simmer, uncovered, 8–10 minutes until almost tender. Drain asparagus and reserve cooking water.

Heat oil in heavy casserole. Add garlic and parsley, and saute 2 minutes. Add fish slices and 1 cup reserved asparagus cooking water. Add lemon juice, Spike, and pepper. Cover and simmer 10 minutes.

Arrange asparagus tips over fish. Cover and continue cooking 10 minutes until cod and asparagus are tender. Serve from casserole.

Serves 4

NUTRITIONAL DATA

PER SERVING

calories	311
protein (gm)	49.5
fat (gm)	8.9
cholesterol (mg)	109
sodium (mg)	161
% calories from fat	26

♥

FISH STEW WITH VEGETABLES AND GARLIC

*T**his dish is a garlic lover's dream. Serve with crusty bread and salad for a wonderful meal anytime of year.*

> 2 tablespoons olive oil
>
> 1 large red onion, peeled, halved, and sliced
>
> 2–3 lbs. small white potatoes, peeled and cut into ½-in. slices
>
> 2 large carrots, pared and cut into 1-in. slices
>
> 1–2 celery ribs, cut into ½-in. pieces
>
> Black pepper, freshly ground to taste
>
> 1 teaspoon basil
>
> 4–6 garlic cloves, chopped
>
> Spike to taste
>
> 2½ lbs. fresh fish fillets, cut into 2-in. squares
>
> ¼ cup fresh lemon juice, strained

In a large heavy pot, heat olive oil and saute onions until translucent. Add potatoes, carrots, celery, and pepper and saute 3–4 minutes, stirring constantly with wooden spoon. Add basil and garlic and enough water to almost cover vegetables. Bring to a boil, reduce heat, season with Spike, cover, and simmer 10–15 minutes until vegetables are about half-cooked.

Add fish and stir gently so fish doesn't fall apart. Simmer, covered, another 10–15 minutes, adding a little water if necessary to keep pot moist, until fish is tender, vegetables are cooked, and most of liquid is absorbed.

Remove lid and pour in lemon juice. Continue to cook 3–5 minutes before taking pot off heat. Season with freshly ground pepper and serve hot.

Serves 6

NUTRITIONAL DATA

PER SERVING		EXCHANGES	
calories	348	milk	0.0
protein (gm)	34.8	vegetable	1.0
fat (gm)	6.7	fruit	0.0
cholesterol (mg)	88	bread	1.5
sodium (mg)	160	meat	4.0
% calories from fat	18	fat	0.0

VEGETABLES

FRENCH VEGETABLES

■

ROSEMARY-SCENTED POTATO GRATIN

10 Idaho baking potatoes, cleaned and peeled
   Vegetable cooking spray
4 cloves garlic, minced
4 shallots, minced
1 handful parsley, chopped
1 tablespoon fresh rosemary, minced
4 tablespoons Parmesan cheese, freshly grated
   Black pepper to taste, freshly ground
2–3 cups chicken stock

Slice potatoes into ⅛-in. or thinner circles. Spray a 12-in. ovenproof gratin dish with vegetable spray. Slightly overlap potato slices in spiral fashion to cover bottom of pan.

In a small mixing bowl, combine garlic, shallots, parsley, rosemary, and freshly grated Parmesan cheese and season with pepper. Sprinkle about ⅓ of mixture over potatoes. Continue to layer potatoes and cheese mixture until pan is three-fourths filled.

Cover with chicken stock, and bake in a preheated 350° oven 45 minutes or until potatoes are cooked. Remove from oven and let cool 5 minutes before serving.

Serves 12

NUTRITIONAL DATA

PER SERVING		EXCHANGES	
calories	132	milk	0.0
protein (gm)	5.4	vegetable	0.0
fat (gm)	2.2	fruit	0.0
cholesterol (mg)	5	bread	1.5
sodium (mg)	251	meat	0.5
% calories from fat	15	fat	0.0

♥

CARROTS VICHY

Everyone I serve this dish to is pleasantly surprised at the combination of carrots and onions. They love it!

1 lb. carrots, scraped and cut into slices ½-in. thick

2½ cups water (divided)

1 teaspoon granulated sugar

1 teaspoon Spike

Vegetable cooking spray

2 large onions, chopped

1 envelope butter buds

2 tablespoons parsley, chopped

In heavy saucepan, combine carrots, water, sugar, and Spike. Cover and bring to boil. Lower flame and simmer 30 minutes. Remove from heat and set aside.

In small skillet sprayed with vegetable spray, add onions and cook until soft. Add carrots and butter buds with ½ cup water. Simmer about 3 minutes. Remove from heat and place carrots in a bowl. Top with parsley.

Serves 4

NUTRITIONAL DATA

PER SERVING		EXCHANGES	
calories	87	milk	0.0
protein (gm)	2.1	vegetable	3.5
fat (gm)	0.4	fruit	0.0
cholesterol (mg)	0	bread	0.0
sodium (mg)	43	meat	0.0
% calories from fat	4	fat	0.0

ARTICHOKE DELIGHT

1 10-oz. package frozen artichokes
Vegetable cooking spray
2 tablespoons shallots, finely chopped
2 tablespoons onions, finely chopped
1 teaspoon Spike
¼ teaspoon black pepper, freshly ground
2 tablespoons white wine vinegar
¼ cup white wine
½ cup boiling water
1 clove garlic, minced
½ bay leaf, crushed

Spray large skillet with vegetable cooking spray and add artichokes, shallots, and onions. Cook over medium heat, turning frequently, for 5 minutes or until artichokes are separated and onions are softened but not browned. Add Spike, pepper, vinegar, and wine. Bring to boil and cook on high for 10 minutes or until liquid is reduced to about 2 tablespoons. Remove artichokes to heated serving dish and keep warm. Add to skillet, boiling water, garlic, and bay leaf. Heat through and pour sauce over artichokes.
    Serves 4

NUTRITIONAL DATA

PER SERVING		EXCHANGES	
calories	52	milk	0.0
protein (gm)	2.7	vegetable	2.0
fat (gm)	0.1	fruit	0.0
cholesterol (mg)	0	bread	0.0
sodium (mg)	69	meat	0.0
% calories from fat	2	fat	0.0

■

PROVENÇAL ROAST TOMATOES

This dish is excellent in summer but also can be used when tomatoes are past their prime.

    8 firm, ripe tomatoes (about 2 lbs.), cored and halved
      crosswise
    Spike
    Black pepper, freshly ground
    8 garlic cloves, minced
    ½ cup fresh breadcrumbs
    10 fresh basil leaves, chopped
    Fresh parsley, handful, chopped

Preheat oven to 400°.

Arrange tomatoes, cut sides up, in large baking dish. Season generously with Spike and pepper. Sprinkle garlic over tomatoes. Combine breadcrumbs, basil, and parsley and spread over tomatoes. Bake, uncovered, until tomatoes are soft and sizzling, about 1 hour. Serve immediately.

Serves 8

NUTRITIONAL DATA

PER SERVING		EXCHANGES	
calories	53	milk	0.0
protein (gm)	2.0	vegetable	2.0
fat (gm)	0.7	fruit	0.0
cholesterol (mg)	0	bread	0.0
sodium (mg)	57	meat	0.0
% calories from fat	11	fat	0.0

♥

ITALIAN VEGETABLES

ITALIAN STRING BEANS

1 lb. string beans, cut in 2-in. pieces

1 tablespoon olive oil

¼ cup seasoned breadcrumbs

¼ cup Parmesan or Romano cheese, freshly grated
  Pepper

6 fresh basil leaves, coarsely chopped

½ cup "Sun-Dried" Tomatoes in Herb Oil (p. 13), or sun-dried tomatoes

Steam string beans 5 minutes and drain. Heat oil in pan and saute beans 3 minutes. Add breadcrumbs, cheese, and pepper. Toss together thoroughly. Garnish with fresh basil and sun-dried tomatoes.

Serves 6

NUTRITIONAL DATA

PER SERVING		EXCHANGES	
calories	107	milk	0.0
protein (gm)	4.8	vegetable	3.0
fat (gm)	4.0	fruit	0.0
cholesterol (mg)	3	bread	0.0
sodium (mg)	122	meat	0.0
% calories from fat	31	fat	0.5

■

VEGETABLE STEW

When I was a child, our neighbor, Mrs. Patrenelli, used to make this on Friday, when Catholics could not eat meat. Everyone loved it.

Vegetable cooking spray

4 cloves garlic, minced

2 onions, sliced

4 carrots, peeled and cut into 1-in. pieces

2 celery stalks, cut in ½-in. pieces

4 medium zucchini, sliced

2 large potatoes, peeled and cut into 1½-in. pieces

2 cups fresh peas

1 18-oz. can stewed tomatoes (salt free)

1 28-oz. can crushed tomatoes (salt free)

Pepper to taste

1 teaspoon oregano

10 leaves fresh basil, coarsely chopped

10-12 mushrooms, sliced

Spray large pan with vegetable cooking spray and add garlic and onions. Saute a few minutes, then add carrots, celery, zucchini, potatoes, and peas. Add both kinds of tomatoes, pepper, oregano, and basil; simmer 40 minutes until carrots are just tender. Add mushrooms and allow stew to cook 2–3 minutes more.

Serves 6

NUTRITIONAL DATA

PER SERVING		EXCHANGES	
calories	178	milk	0.0
protein (gm)	7.6	vegetable	4.0
fat (gm)	1.1	fruit	0.0
cholesterol (mg)	0	bread	1.0
sodium (mg)	64	meat	0.0
% calories from fat	5	fat	0.0

♥

TOMATOES STUFFED WITH MUSHROOMS, OLIVES, AND EGGPLANT

S erve this as a hot side dish with an entree, or serve it as an appetizer.

4 large, fresh tomatoes

Vegetable cooking spray

½ lb. fresh mushrooms, diced

1 medium onion, chopped

3 cloves garlic, crushed

1 medium-size eggplant

1 teaspoon dried basil

6 black olives, sliced

½ cup parsley, chopped

½ cup seasoned breadcrumbs

Preheat oven to 350°.

Scoop out center of tomatoes and put them aside.

Spray large skillet with vegetable cooking spray and add mushrooms, onion, garlic, and eggplant. Saute over medium heat 10 minutes. Add tomato pulp, basil, olives, and parsley. Cook together 5 minutes.

Place tomato shells in baking dish sprayed with vegetable cooking spray. Fill each shell with sauteed mixture. Sprinkle each with breadcrumbs and bake 10 minutes.

Serves 4

NUTRITIONAL DATA

PER SERVING		EXCHANGES	
calories	117	milk	0.0
protein (gm)	4.7	vegetable	2.0
fat (gm)	2.4	fruit	0.0
cholesterol (mg)	0	bread	0.5
sodium (mg)	139	meat	0.0
% calories from fat	17	fat	0.5

♥

ZUCCHINI ITALIANO

Vegetable cooking spray

1 medium-size onion, chopped

6 medium zucchini, sliced

2 cloves garlic, minced

1 14½-oz. can chunky tomatoes

4 fresh basil leaves, coarsely chopped

¼ teaspoon red pepper flakes

Spray 10-in. skillet with cooking spray and add onion. Saute about 10 minutes. Add zucchini and garlic and saute another 10 minutes. Add tomatoes, basil, and pepper, and cook another 5 minutes.

Serves 6

NUTRITIONAL DATA

PER SERVING		EXCHANGES	
calories	39	milk	0.0
protein (gm)	2.4	vegetable	1.5
fat (gm)	0.4	fruit	0.0
cholesterol (mg)	0	bread	0.0
sodium (mg)	116	meat	0.0
% calories from fat	7	fat	0.0

GREEK VEGETABLES

VEGETABLES À LA GRECQUE

The Greeks love marinated vegetables and serve them often. You can prepare 2 pounds of string beans or an assortment of whatever vegetables you have on hand. I like to make an assortment, but be sure to cook each group separately so you can control the degree of tenderness desired. These look lovely if arranged creatively, giving thought to color and texture.

  1 cup dry white wine
  1 recipe Italian Dressing (p. 55)
  1 large celery stalk with leaves, washed and peeled
  2 stalks fresh fennel, or ½ teaspoon fennel seeds
  2 sprigs fresh thyme, or ½ teaspoon dried thyme
  10 peppercorns, cracked
  12 coriander seeds, cracked
  2 lbs. vegetables (string beans or assortment)

Combine all ingredients except 2 lbs. vegetables in 4-qt. pot and bring to boil. Cover pot, reduce heat, and simmer 1 hour. Strain cooked marinade through cheesecloth or fine sieve into a bowl and press down to extract every last bit of taste before discarding vegetables and spices.

Pour clear marinade back into pot. Wash and trim vegetables you're using and simmer in marinade until tender. Lift out with slotted spoon and arrange artfully on platter.

Boil marinade down to 1 cup. Pour marinade over vegetables and allow to cool. Cover and refrigerate 6–12 hours.
Serves 6

NUTRITIONAL DATA

PER SERVING		EXCHANGES	
calories	82	milk	0.0
protein (gm)	2.2	vegetable	3.0
fat (gm)	0.5	fruit	0.0
cholesterol (mg)	0	bread	0.0
sodium (mg)	18	meat	0.0
% calories from fat	5	fat	0.0

GREEK COUNTRY BEANS

1 lb. dried beans (navy, white, broad, or lima)

Vegetable cooking spray

2 large onions, chopped

2 cloves garlic, minced

½ cup Light Tomato Sauce (p. 228)

2 carrots, diced

2 celery stalks, diced

1½ teaspoons Spike

½ teaspoon black pepper, freshly ground

1 teaspoon sugar

½ cup parsley, chopped

1 teaspoon oregano

Soak beans overnight in water to cover. (Or cover beans with 2½ cups cold water, bring to boil, boil 2 minutes, and let stand 1 hour.) Drain.

Spray 3-qt. saucepan with vegetable cooking spray and saute onions and garlic 10 minutes over medium heat until golden. Add remaining ingredients and saute another 10 minutes.

Add beans and enough boiling water to barely cover beans (about 1½ cups). Stir once to mix, cover, and simmer until vegetables and beans are very tender, about 1¼ hours.

Serves 6

NUTRITIONAL DATA

PER SERVING		EXCHANGES	
calories	289	milk	0.0
protein (gm)	16.4	vegetable	3.0
fat (gm)	1.2	fruit	0.0
cholesterol (mg)	0	bread	3.0
sodium (mg)	149	meat	0.0
% calories from fat	4	fat	0.0

SPANISH VEGETABLES

GREEN PEAS VALENCIA STYLE

This is an elegant version of stewed green peas. White wine and saffron make it special.

Vegetable cooking spray
1 medium onion, finely chopped
2 cloves garlic, minced
1 small yellow bell pepper, minced
½ lb. shelled green peas, defrosted if frozen
¼ cup white wine
¼ cup water
2 tablespoons fresh parsley, chopped
1 tablespoon fresh thyme, chopped
1 bay leaf, crushed
Pepper, freshly ground
⅛ teaspoon saffron threads
Pimiento strips for garnish

Spray skillet with vegetable cooking spray and saute onions and garlic about 3 minutes. Stir in bell pepper, peas, wine, and water. Add herbs and pepper and bring to simmer; cover and cook over low heat until peas are tender, 15–20 minutes, or a shorter time if peas are frozen. Stir in saffron threads and cook a few minutes longer. Serve garnished with pimiento.

Serves 4

NUTRITIONAL DATA

PER SERVING		EXCHANGES	
calories	71	milk	0.0
protein (gm)	3.5	vegetable	1.0
fat (gm)	0.2	fruit	0.0
cholesterol (mg)	0	bread	0.5
sodium (mg)	52	meat	0.0
% calories from fat	3	fat	0.0

BRAISED SPRING VEGETABLES

2 tablespoons olive oil

4 spring onions (scallions), trimmed and sliced, using some of green parts

3 tomatoes, peeled and chopped

2 small carrots, scraped and sliced

2 small turnips, peeled and sliced

4 ozs. cured ham, cut into strips

½ lb. green beans, halved

4 artichoke hearts (canned)

½ lb. fresh peas, shelled

8 small new potatoes

2 cups beef stock

Pepper, freshly ground

8 asparagus tips

Heat oil in 4-qt. pot and saute spring onions and tomatoes until mixture is thick and blended well. Add carrots, turnips, ham, green beans, artichoke hearts, peas, and new potatoes and cook 5 minutes longer. Pour in stock, season with pepper, cover, and cook 10 minutes longer or until all vegetables are tender. Garnish with asparagus tips.

Serves 4

NUTRITIONAL DATA

PER SERVING		EXCHANGES	
calories	344	milk	0.0
protein (gm)	16.4	vegetable	2.0
fat (gm)	9.4	fruit	0.0
cholesterol (mg)	8	bread	2.0
sodium (mg)	578	meat	1.0
% calories from fat	23	fat	2.0

MOROCCAN VEGETABLES

☆

MOROCCAN CARROTS

8 medium carrots

2 teaspoons paprika

½ teaspoon cinnamon

¼ teaspoon black pepper, freshly ground

1 teaspoon ground cumin

2 tablespoons fresh lemon juice

1 tablespoon sugar

⅓ cup Vinaigrette (p. 50)

2 onions, chopped and sauteed, kept warm

Peel carrots and thinly slice or cut into julienne strips. Place in bowl. Put spices, lemon juice, and sugar in mortar and grind with pestle to emulsify. Gradually work in vinaigrette. Pour dressing over carrots and toss. Add onions and toss again.

Serves 4

NUTRITIONAL DATA

PER SERVING		EXCHANGES	
calories	104	milk	0.0
protein (gm)	2.4	vegetable	4.0
fat (gm)	0.5	fruit	0.0
cholesterol (mg)	0	bread	0.0
sodium (mg)	53	meat	0.0
% calories from fat	4	fat	0.0

♥

BEANS, RICE, & GRAINS

FRENCH BEANS, RICE, AND GRAINS

RICE MALGACHE

Vegetable cooking spray
2 tablespoons shallots, chopped
1 green bell pepper, chopped
1 cup long-grain rice
1 teaspoon Spike
Pinch of saffron
1 cup consommé
2 cups boiling water

Spray large, heavy saucepan with vegetable cooking spray; add shallots and pepper. Cook until browned. Add rice and cook, stirring constantly, until rice is well coated. Add Spike, saffron, consommé, and water. Bring to boil. Cover and simmer 15 minutes or until rice has absorbed all liquid. Serve hot or cold.
Serves 6

NUTRITIONAL DATA

PER SERVING		EXCHANGES	
calories	121	milk	0.0
protein (gm)	3.2	vegetable	0.0
fat (gm)	0.2	fruit	0.0
cholesterol (mg)	0	bread	1.5
sodium (mg)	108	meat	0.0
% calories from fat	2	fat	0.0

♥

COUSCOUS NIÇOISE

This is a colorful accompaniment to roast chicken or poached fish. If you add a little more vinegar, you can also serve it as a salad.

1¼ cups chicken stock

2 cloves garlic, minced

1½ teaspoons olive oil

1½ cups medium-grain instant couscous

8 cherry tomatoes, cut in half

¼ cup Niçoise olives,* sliced

8 leaves fresh basil, cut julienne

1 tablespoon parsley, minced

1 tablespoon red wine vinegar

1 tablespoon chives, minced

Pepper, freshly ground

Combine stock, garlic, and oil in medium-size saucepan with tight-fitting lid and bring to boil. Stir in couscous and remove from heat. Cover and let stand 5 minutes. Uncover and fluff with fork until grains are separate.

Add tomatoes, olives, basil, parsley, vinegar, and chives. Toss until completely mixed. Season with freshly ground black pepper. Serve warm or at room temperature.

Serves 6

NUTRITIONAL DATA

PER SERVING		EXCHANGES	
calories	199	milk	0.0
protein (gm)	7.1	vegetable	0.0
fat (gm)	2.2	fruit	0.0
cholesterol (mg)	0	bread	2.5
sodium (mg)	181	meat	0.0
% calories from fat	10	fat	0.5

♥

*Note: Niçoise olives are found in specialty stores, or substitute Italian or Greek olives.

WHITE BEANS À LA PROVENÇAL

White beans go beautifully with tomatoes, garlic, thyme, and basil—such a lovely combination of Provençal flavors.

½ lb. dried white beans (Great Northern, navy, or small white), washed and picked over

2 tablespoons olive oil divided

1 red onion, chopped

2 garlic cloves, minced (divided)

1 qt. water

1 bay leaf

Spike

1 14½-oz. can chunky tomatoes, or 3 fresh, chopped

1 teaspoon fresh thyme, or ¼ teaspoon dried

2 tablespoons fresh basil, chopped

Black pepper, freshly ground

2 tablespoons fresh parsley, chopped

If you're using dried beans, soak in 1 qt. water overnight or for several hours, and drain. Heat 1 tablespoon oil in large, heavy saucepan and saute onion and 1 clove of garlic until onion is tender. Add beans along with 1 qt. water and bay leaf. Bring to boil, reduce heat, cover, and simmer 1½ hours or until beans are tender. Add Spike to taste, remove bay leaf, drain, and save cooking liquid.

Heat remaining oil in skillet and saute remaining garlic over medium heat 1 minute. Add tomatoes, thyme, and basil and simmer 10 minutes. Add beans, ½ cup cooking liquid, and cover. Simmer 10 more minutes. Remove from heat and stir in pepper to taste and parsley.

Serves 4 (as side dish)

NUTRITIONAL DATA

PER SERVING		EXCHANGES	
calories	287	milk	0.0
protein (gm)	13.5	vegetable	2.0
fat (gm)	7.9	fruit	0.0
cholesterol (mg)	0	bread	2.0
sodium (mg)	172	meat	0.0
% calories from fat	24	fat	2.0

♥

JU92

BRAISED RICE

Vegetable cooking spray

⅓ cup onions, finely minced

1 cup raw white rice, unwashed (Carolina long-grain works well)

¼ cup dry white French vermouth

2 cups chicken stock, heated in small saucepan

Pepper, freshly ground

1 medium bay leaf

1 bouquet garni*

Spray skillet with cooking spray and add onions. Saute onions slowly for several minutes until soft. Stir in rice, and saute, slowly stirring for several minutes more until grains, which first become translucent, turn milky white. This step prevents grains from sticking.

Stir in vermouth and let it boil down for a moment. Blend in chicken stock, correct the seasoning, and add bay leaf and bouquet garni. Bring to simmer, stir to keep from sticking, and let rice cook, covered, for about 20 minutes. Remove from heat; remove bay leaf and bouquet garni; and serve.

Makes 3 cups.

Serves 6

NUTRITIONAL DATA

PER SERVING		EXCHANGES	
calories	139	milk	0.0
protein (gm)	3.9	vegetable	0.0
fat (gm)	0.7	fruit	0.0
cholesterol (mg)	0	bread	2.0
sodium (mg)	261	meat	0.0
% calories from fat	5	fat	0.0

*Note: Bouquet garni consists of a few sprigs of parsley, thyme, and basil or tarragon with a bay leaf, all in a cheesecloth bag.

ITALIAN BEANS, RICE, AND GRAINS

■

SEAFOOD RISOTTO WITH TOMATOES

5-6 cups chicken stock (homemade or low-sodium)

3 tablespoons olive oil

1¾ lbs. crabmeat, picked over for cartilage and broken into large pieces; or bay or sea scallops; or medium shrimp, shelled and deveined

Spike

Pepper, freshly ground

1 envelope butter buds mixed in ½ cup skim milk, warmed

1½ cups onions, diced

2 cups arborio rice

3 cups Italian plum tomatoes, drained and diced, juices added to chicken stock

6 artichoke hearts, canned

2 tablespoons garlic, finely minced

3 tablespoons lemon zest

2 tablespoons lemon juice

8 fresh basil leaves, chopped

¼ cup fresh parsley, chopped, plus additional for garnish

Heat chicken stock to boiling in saucepan; reduce heat and hold at simmer.

Heat olive oil in large saute pan over medium heat. Sprinkle shellfish with Spike and pepper. Add shellfish to pan and saute quickly.

Put butter buds and milk in heavy saucepan over low heat. Add onions and cook about 5 minutes. Add rice and cook, stirring to coat with butter buds mixture. Add ½ cup hot stock and cook, stirring constantly, until stock is absorbed. Continue, adding stock ½ cup at a time, and stirring until rice is almost completely cooked. Add tomatoes, artichoke hearts, garlic, lemon zest, lemon juice, basil, and parsley. Continue to cook.

A minute or two before rice is cooked, add shellfish. Season with Spike and pepper and sprinkle with a little more parsley.

Serves 6

NUTRITIONAL DATA

PER SERVING		EXCHANGES	
calories	413	milk	0.0
protein (gm)	15.9	vegetable	2.0
fat (gm)	9.6	fruit	0.0
cholesterol (mg)	21	bread	3.0
sodium (mg)	453	meat	2.0
% calories from fat	21	fat	1.0

♥

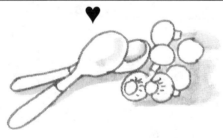

BASIC POLENTA

Cornmeal is plentiful, cheap, and easy to pre-pare. It can be mixed with almost anything: vegetables, game, mushrooms, or just a little cheese. It can be served as an appetizer or main course, with eggs or tomatoes. (See "Variations" at bottom of page.)

2½ qts. cold water

½ lb. yellow cornmeal, coarse or stone-ground

½ lb. yellow cornmeal (regular type), finely ground

Dash black pepper

Bring cold water to boil in large pot. Add two types of cornmeal to boiling water in very slow stream; stir with wooden spoon to keep mixture smooth or it will become lumpy. Stir slowly about 30 minutes. If lumps form, push them to side of pot and smash with spoon. Add pepper to taste. Serve immediately.

Serves 6

NUTRITIONAL DATA

PER SERVING		EXCHANGES	
calories	274	milk	0.0
protein (gm)	6.1	vegetable	0.0
fat (gm)	2.7	fruit	0.0
cholesterol (mg)	0	bread	4.0
sodium (mg)	26	meat	0.0
% calories from fat	9	fat	0.0

Variations: Add grated Parmesan cheese if serving with game or meats. If polenta is baked or used as an appetizer, remove it from pot by scraping it from the sides and bottom. Pour polenta onto a smooth surface that is covered with foil. Spread it out with a spatula. When cold, you can cut the polenta into different shapes for appetizers.

GREEN RISOTTO

1 10-oz. package frozen chopped spinach

2 tablespoons olive oil

1 medium onion, chopped

1 garlic clove, minced

2 cups raw rice

4 cups chicken stock (homemade or low sodium)

1 teaspoon Spike

¼ cup Parmesan cheese, freshly grated

Drain spinach well. Combine spinach, olive oil, onion, and garlic in heavy saucepan. Bring to boil; cook, stirring constantly, about 5 minutes.

Press through fine sieve or blend smooth in blender; return to pan. Add rice, stock, and Spike; cover.

Cook over low heat until liquid is absorbed and rice is tender, about 20 minutes. Stir occasionally. If rice is not tender, add a little water; cook until rice is soft. Serve immediately, topped with grated cheese.

Serves 6

NUTRITIONAL DATA

PER SERVING		EXCHANGES	
calories	325	milk	0.0
protein (gm)	9.4	vegetable	1.0
fat (gm)	7.3	fruit	0.0
cholesterol (mg)	6	bread	3.0
sodium (mg)	158	meat	0.5
% calories from fat	20	fat	1.0

■

RISOTTO PRIMAVERA PARMIGIANA

I talian rice with vegetables, tomatoes, and cheese makes a very inexpensive dish that is wonderful, and you can vary it greatly. So serve it often. And it's a good source of complex carbohydrates.

6 shallots, or 1 large onion, diced

2 cloves garlic, minced

½ teaspoon crushed red pepper

2 cups mixed vegetables, diced (zucchini, broccoli, mushrooms, bell peppers, asparagus, eggplant, green peas, spinach, green beans, yellow squash)

2 tablespoons olive oil

1 teaspoon oregano

1 teaspoon basil

1 teaspoon thyme

2½ cups arborio rice

2 cups Italian plum tomatoes with juice, crushed

1 cup warm water

8 fresh basil leaves, sliced thin

1 cup fresh Italian parsley, chopped

½ cup Parmesan cheese, freshly grated

Preheat oven to 350°. In large casserole that can be used for serving, saute shallots, garlic, red pepper, and vegetables in olive oil for a few minutes, stirring often. Add herbs and rice. Add crushed tomatoes with water and stir well until rice is cooked, about 20 minutes, and liquid is absorbed. Add basil, parsley, and Parmesan cheese and stir well. Serve immediately, or bake, covered, for about 5 minutes before serving.

Serves 6

NUTRITIONAL DATA

PER SERVING		EXCHANGES	
calories	411	milk	0.0
protein (gm)	11.4	vegetable	1.0
fat (gm)	8.0	fruit	0.0
cholesterol (mg)	6	bread	4.5
sodium (mg)	251	meat	0.5
% calories from fat	18	fat	1.0

GREEK BEANS, RICE, AND GRAINS

LENTIL AND RICE PILAF

1 cup dried lentils, washed

4½ cups water

1 bay leaf

1 small chili pepper, minced

1 garlic clove, minced

1 cup plum tomatoes, peeled and chopped

2 tablespoons olive oil

1 onion, chopped

¾ cup long-grain rice

In medium-size saucepan, bring lentils and water to rolling boil over high heat. Add bay leaf, chili pepper, garlic, and tomatoes. Simmer, covered, about 35 minutes. Stir occasionally with wooden spoon, until lentils are softened.

While lentils simmer, heat 2 tablespoons of oil in large skillet, and saute onion until translucent. When lentils are softened, add rice and onions to pot and simmer 20 minutes longer, until rice is cooked. Add more water if necessary, and stir occasionally to keep mixture from sticking to bottom of pan. Remove from heat. Discard bay leaf and mix well. Serve warm.

Serves 6

NUTRITIONAL DATA

PER SERVING		EXCHANGES	
calories	216	milk	0.0
protein (gm)	8.1	vegetable	1.0
fat (gm)	5.0	fruit	0.0
cholesterol (mg)	0	bread	2.0
sodium (mg)	5	meat	0.0
% calories from fat	21	fat	1.0

RICE IN YOGURT SAUCE

2 cups plain low-fat yogurt, strained 30 minutes in double thickness of cheesecloth

Egg substitute = to 1 egg

1 teaspoon dried mint, or 3 teaspoons fresh mint, chopped

1 garlic clove, minced

Spike to taste

Pepper, freshly ground, to taste

¼ cup pimiento, chopped

1 cup long-grain rice, cooked

In medium-size bowl, stir together all ingredients except rice. Pour yogurt mixture over cooked rice.

Serves 4

NUTRITIONAL DATA

PER SERVING		EXCHANGES	
calories	123	milk	0.0
protein (gm)	7.5	vegetable	0.0
fat (gm)	0.7	fruit	0.0
cholesterol (mg)	3	bread	1.0
sodium (mg)	78	meat	1.0
% calories from fat	4	fat	0.0

SPANISH BEANS, RICE, AND GRAIN

PAELLA VALENCIANA

This is a wonderful party dish. It evokes conversation, and people love it.

12 clams

12 mussels

2 tablespoons olive oil

1 cup onion, chopped

2 green bell peppers, chopped

1 clove garlic, minced

1 lb. boneless chicken breast, cut into small pieces

2 large tomatoes, seeded and chopped

1½ cups long-grain rice

Large pinch saffron threads, soaked in 1 tablespoon water

1 teaspoon Spike

2 cups liquid from steaming clams and mussels

1 lb. jumbo shrimp, cleaned and deveined

1 package frozen green peas, thawed

1 can artichoke hearts

½ cup roasted peppers

2 ozs. pimiento

½ cup parsley, chopped

1 large lemon, cut into slices

Scrub clams and mussels thoroughly. Place about 1 in. of water in deep pot. Bring to boil. Add clams and mussels. Cover and steam 7–8 minutes or until shells open. Remove shellfish from broth and set aside. Strain liquid into 2-cup measure and reserve. Add chicken broth if necessary to make 2 cups.

Add oil to paella pot with chopped onion, green peppers, garlic, and chicken. Saute about 5 minutes, stirring often. When chicken is opaque, add tomatoes, rice, and saffron with its soaking water. Add Spike and pour in reserved 2 cups of broth. Bring to boil, stir once, and reduce heat so liquid simmers very slowly.

After 10 minutes, add shrimp, pushing them down among other ingredients. After 5 minutes, add peas, artichoke hearts, roasted peppers, and pimiento. Cook about 5 more minutes.

Before adding mussels and clams, cover pot and let sit 5 minutes. Sprinkle with parsley and arrange lemon slices on top.

Serves 6

NUTRITIONAL DATA

PER SERVING		EXCHANGES	
calories	510	milk	0.0
protein (gm)	46.0	vegetable	1.5
fat (gm)	11.0	fruit	0.0
cholesterol (mg)	187	bread	3.0
sodium (mg)	338	meat	4.0
% calories from fat	19	fat	1.0

BLACK BEANS AND RICE

T*his is a colonial Spanish dish from Cuba.*

1¼ cups black (turtle) beans

2 cups water

2 tablespoons olive oil

1 medium onion, finely chopped

1 clove garlic, minced

½ medium-sweet green pepper, seeded and chopped

2 large tomatoes, peeled, seeded, and chopped

Spike

Pepper, freshly ground

1 cup short-grain rice

Put beans to soak in covering cold water in large saucepan 1–2 hours. Drain. Return beans to pan with 2 cups cold water, bring to simmer, and cook, covered, over low heat until beans are tender, 1½ hours. Check to see if beans need more water to keep from drying out, and add a little boiling water if necessary.

While beans are cooking, heat oil in skillet and saute onion, garlic, and pepper until onion is soft. Add tomatoes and cook until mixture is smooth and well blended. Season with Spike and pepper.

Drain beans and add tomato mixture, stirring to mix. Add rice and water, stir gently, cover, and cook over very low heat until rice is tender and all liquid absorbed. Serve with Light Tomato Sauce (p. 228).

Serves 6

NUTRITIONAL DATA

PER SERVING		EXCHANGES	
calories	256	milk	0.0
protein (gm)	9.2	vegetable	1.0
fat (gm)	5.3	fruit	0.0
cholesterol (mg)	0	bread	4.0
sodium (mg)	6	meat	0.0
% calories from fat	18	fat	0.0

♥

MOROCCAN BEANS, RICE, AND GRAIN

☆

COUSCOUS WITH SEVEN VEGETABLES

Couscous is the national dish of Morocco. There, it is less spicy than versions now found in France. This is a one-pot meal, easy to make for large numbers.

VEGETABLES

½ lb. chickpeas, soaked at least 1 hour, or canned chickpeas

2 large onions, quartered, then thickly sliced

3 garlic cloves, minced

½ teaspoon saffron

2 teaspoons cinnamon

1 teaspoon paprika

Large pinch cayenne (optional)

½ teaspoon ground ginger

Spike to taste

7 vegetables (plus raisins) chosen from:

1 lb. carrots, cut up

1 medium white cabbage, cut into 8 pieces

6 artichoke hearts

2 medium eggplants, quartered

1 lb. small potatoes

1 lb. turnips, quartered

1 lb. broad beans, shelled

8 oz. raisins (preferably large Malaga)

1 lb. of orange pumpkin, cut into pieces

4 tomatoes, quartered

Large bunch parsley, chopped

COUSCOUS

2 cups couscous

3 cups water, or seasoned broth

1 teaspoon Spike

1 tablespoon diet margarine

Vegetables:

Put chickpeas in large pot. Cover with water (5 pts.) and bring to boil, removing froth. Add onion, garlic, and spices and simmer at least 1 hour. Add Spike when chickpeas begin to soften.

Add carrots, cabbage, artichoke hearts, eggplants, and potatoes. Add more water if necessary, and cook 20 minutes. Add turnips, broad beans, and raisins and cook 10 minutes more. Add pumpkin and tomatoes and after 5 minutes, while they are still firm, add parsley and cook 5 minutes longer.

While vegetables are cooking, prepare couscous as described below, putting it to steam when turnips, broad beans, and raisins are added.

Couscous:

In saucepan, bring water, Spike, and margarine to boil. Stir in couscous; cover. Remove from heat and let steam 5 minutes. Turn out couscous onto large, round serving dish and crush with fork to separate grains. Stir in any oil and ladle on a little vegetable broth—just enough to moisten it. Then shape into a mound with a well in the center.

Lift vegetables out, using perforated spoon, place them in the well, and serve at once with the broth in separate bowl. If you expect to have left-over couscous, serve vegetables in separate bowl so that you can reheat couscous.

Serves 12

NUTRITIONAL DATA

PER SERVING		EXCHANGES	
calories	527	milk	0.0
protein (gm)	18.7	vegetable	3.0
fat (gm)	2.2	fruit	1.5
cholesterol (mg)	0	bread	5.0
sodium (mg)	85	meat	0.0
% calories from fat	4	fat	0.0

PASTA

JH92

FRENCH PASTA

FRENCH SPAGHETTI

*L*ayers *of white sauce and tomato-mushroom sauce top French Spaghetti. This meatless main dish is excellent with a salad and fruit for dessert.*

Vegetable cooking spray
1¼ cups green peppers, chopped
1 onion, chopped
3 shallots, chopped
1 lb. whole tomatoes, cut up
1 tablespoon fresh basil, chopped
1 teaspoon fresh tarragon, chopped
1 teaspoon fresh thyme, chopped
½ cup mushrooms, sliced
¼ cup ripe olives, sliced
1 tablespoon diet margarine
4 teaspoons all-purpose flour
¾ cup evaporated skim milk
¾ cup skim milk
1 lb. spaghetti, cooked
¼ cup Parmesan cheese, freshly grated

Spray 10-in. skillet with vegetable cooking spray and add peppers, onion, and shallots. Saute till tender. Stir in undrained tomatoes and bring to boil. Reduce heat and simmer, uncovered, for 2 hours. Add herbs and simmer another 10 minutes. Stir in mushrooms and olives.

To make white sauce, melt margarine in saucepan and stir in flour. Add evaporated skim milk and skim milk all at once. Cook and stir till thickened and bubbly. Remove from heat.

To assemble, arrange spaghetti in 8x8x2-in. baking dish. Top with white sauce, then tomato-mushroom sauce. Sprinkle with Parmesan. Bake, uncovered, in 350° oven about 25 minutes or until heated through.

Serves 6

NUTRITIONAL DATA

PER SERVING		EXCHANGES	
calories	402	milk	0.5
protein (gm)	16.8	vegetable	1.0
fat (gm)	4.1	fruit	0.0
cholesterol (mg)	5	bread	4.0
sodium (mg)	162	meat	1.0
% calories from fat	9	fat	0.0

PASTA WITH TOMATO, EGGPLANT, AND BELL PEPPER SAUCE

2 tablespoons olive oil

10 medium tomatoes (about 2 lbs.), peeled, cored, seeded, and coarsely chopped

1 large eggplant, unpeeled, cut into bite-size cubes

4 large red bell peppers, cored, seeded, and cut into bite-size pieces

½ teaspoon hot pepper flakes

1 tablespoon *herbes de Provençe*

1 lb. rotini, or tubular pasta

Heat olive oil in large, deep-sided skillet over medium-high heat. Add tomatoes and eggplant. Saute about 10 minutes, stirring from time to time. Add bell peppers and season with pepper flakes and *herbes de Provençe*. Cover and simmer gently about 1 hour.

Just before serving, bring a large pot of water to rolling boil. Add pasta and cook just until tender. Drain.

To serve, divide pasta evenly among dinner plates. Spoon sauce over pasta, allowing each diner to toss the pasta when served.

Serves 6

NUTRITIONAL DATA

PER SERVING		EXCHANGES	
calories	360	milk	0.0
protein (gm)	12.5	vegetable	2.0
fat (gm)	7.4	fruit	0.0
cholesterol (mg)	65	bread	3.5
sodium (mg)	32	meat	0.0
% calories from fat	18	fat	1.5

■■

PASTA WITH CREAMY PESTO

This version of pesto substitutes milk for the usual olive oil.

> 2 cups fresh basil leaves, loosely packed
> 1 cup evaporated skim milk
> 1 lb. tagliatelle, or fettuccine
> ½ cup Parmesan cheese, freshly grated

In food processor or blender, chop basil. Add milk and process to blend. Place creamy basil sauce in large bowl in which you will serve the pasta.

Bring large pot of water to rolling boil. Add pasta and cook just until tender. Drain.

Just before serving, stir Parmesan cheese into the sauce and blend thoroughly. Add pasta to bowl, toss, and serve.

Serves 4

NUTRITIONAL DATA

PER SERVING		EXCHANGES	
calories	496	milk	0.5
protein (gm)	25.0	vegetable	0.0
fat (gm)	7.0	fruit	0.0
cholesterol (mg)	110	bread	5.0
sodium (mg)	324	meat	1.0
% calories from fat	13	fat	1.0

♥

PASTA WITH LEMON, MUSSELS, AND BLACK OLIVES

¼ cup lemon juice, freshly squeezed

¼ cup wine vinegar

¼ cup unsweetened apple juice

2 shallots, cut into rings

½ cup oil-cured black olives, pitted

2 teaspoons fresh thyme

Zest of 2 lemons, grated

Black pepper, coarsely ground

1 lb. thin pasta, such as angel hair or capellini

2 lbs. fresh mussels

Pour lemon juice into small bowl. To complete sauce, add vinegar, apple juice, and shallots. Set aside.

In large, shallow serving bowl, combine olives, thyme, and lemon zest. Season with pepper and toss to blend.

Bring a large pot of water to rolling boil. Add pasta and cook just until tender. Drain. Add pasta to ingredients in serving bowl.

Meanwhile, thoroughly scrub mussels and rinse. Beard mussels (do not do this in advance or they will die and spoil). Place mussels in large, shallow skillet and cover. Turn heat to high and cook, covered, just until mussels open, 2–3 minutes; do not overcook. Remove from heat, discarding any mussels that didn't open.

Remove mussels from shells and add to pasta. Add sauce; toss.

Serves 6

NUTRITIONAL DATA

PER SERVING		EXCHANGES	
calories	372	milk	0.0
protein (gm)	23.7	vegetable	0.0
fat (gm)	5.3	fruit	0.0
cholesterol (mg)	97	bread	2.0
sodium (mg)	247	meat	3.0
% calories from fat	13	fat	0.0

ITALIAN PASTA

PASTA WITH FRESH SEAFOOD SAUCE

1 lb. linguine

1 medium-size onion

2 cloves garlic, minced

2 tablespoons olive oil

½ cup dry white wine

2 cups fresh tomatoes, peeled, seeded, and diced

1 teaspoon oregano

1 tablespoon basil

1 teaspoon thyme

1 cup Italian parsley, chopped

3 cups fresh seafood, chopped (calamari, mussels, clams, shrimp, crabmeat, lobster, cod, bass, or sword-fish)

In large pot, boil water to cook the pasta.

In large skillet, saute onion and garlic in olive oil 2 minutes; add white wine and continue cooking. After 5 more minutes, add tomatoes and herbs with parsley; cook 5 more minutes. Add diced seafood and cook 3–4 more minutes. (Do not overcook seafood.) Remove from heat.

Cook pasta and drain. Place pasta in large bowl; mix in seafood sauce. Serve immediately.

Serves 6

NUTRITIONAL DATA

PER SERVING		EXCHANGES	
calories	411	milk	0.0
protein (gm)	25.0	vegetable	1.0
fat (gm)	8.0	fruit	0.0
cholesterol (mg)	126	bread	3.5
sodium (mg)	353	meat	1.5
% calories from fat	18	fat	1.5

♥

ROTINI WITH VEGETABLES AND CHICKEN

This can be served hot or as a pasta salad.

1 lb. rotini pasta (white or colored)

¼ cup fresh green onion, shallots, or red onion, diced

3 cloves garlic, minced

1 medium yellow bell pepper, chopped

2 tablespoons olive oil

1 cup cooked chicken, diced

1 tablespoon basil

1 teaspoon oregano

1 teaspoon thyme

1 cup frozen peas

½ cup black olives, sliced

1 cup fresh tomatoes, diced

6 fresh basil leaves, chopped, or 1 teaspoon dried basil

1 cup marinated artichoke hearts, quartered

1 cup canned asparagus, cut into 2-in. pieces

1 tablespoon vegetable oil

2 tablespoons balsamic vinegar, or red wine vinegar

½ cup mozzarella cheese, shredded

Boil water and cook pasta.

In large skillet, saute onion, garlic, and pepper in olive oil 4 or 5 minutes. Add chicken and herbs; cook 5 minutes more, stirring often. Add peas, cover, and cook 3–4 minutes more.

Drain cooked pasta and rinse in cold water. If serving hot, turn pasta into serving bowl and top with chicken mixture. If serving as a pasta salad, place pasta in large bowl, add chicken mixture and olives, tomatoes, basil, artichoke hearts, asparagus, vegetable oil, vinegar, and cheese. Mix well.

Serves 6

NUTRITIONAL DATA

PER SERVING		EXCHANGES	
calories	453	milk	0.0
protein (gm)	23.2	vegetable	1.5
fat (gm)	14.7	fruit	0.0
cholesterol (mg)	90	bread	3.0
sodium (mg)	325	meat	2.0
% calories from fat	29	fat	2.0

♥

PASTA WITH WILD MUSHROOMS, PEAS, AND DRIED TOMATOES

1 lb. thin spaghetti

2 ozs. dried porcini mushrooms (soaked in water ½ hour)

1 tablespoon olive oil

1 cup onion, chopped

1 tablespoon fresh basil

1 tablespoon fresh oregano

1 cup fresh or frozen peas

1 cup "Sun-Dried" Tomatoes in Herb Oil (p. 13), or
½ cup purchased sun-dried tomatoes, diced

3 cloves garlic, minced

Dash black pepper

¼ cup Parmesan cheese, freshly grated

½ cup fresh Italian parsley, chopped

Boil water and cook the pasta.

Dry the presoaked mushrooms. In large skillet, combine mushrooms, olive oil, onion, herbs, peas, dried tomatoes, garlic, and pepper and saute 5 minutes over medium heat, stirring often.

Drain pasta, and place it in large pasta bowl. Add Parmesan cheese and parsley. Add sauce and mix thoroughly. Serve immediately.

Serves 6

NUTRITIONAL DATA

PER SERVING		EXCHANGES	
calories	444	milk	0.0
protein (gm)	16.1	vegetable	1.0
fat (gm)	5.2	fruit	0.0
cholesterol (mg)	3	bread	5.0
sodium (mg)	106	meat	0.0
% calories from fat	10	fat	1.0

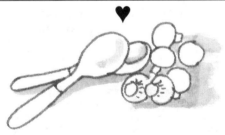

STUFFED SHELLS

This makes an excellent buffet dish. Just add bread, a salad, and dessert.

1 qt. Marinara Sauce (p. 222)

3 egg whites

1 lb. low-fat cottage cheese

1 cup part-skim mozzarella cheese, shredded

4 tablespoons fresh parsley, chopped

10 fresh basil leaves

Dash pepper

24 giant ziti shells

Parmesan cheese to garnish, freshly grated

Make Marinara Sauce and put aside.

In large bowl, combine egg whites, cottage cheese, mozzarella cheese, parsley, basil, and pepper.

Cook giant shells in boiling water until *al dente.* Don't overcook because if ziti are too limp, it's hard to fill them. Drain and stuff each shell with a few tablespoons of cheese mixture.

Cover bottom of large baking dish with about ½ in. of Marinara Sauce. Arrange stuffed shells side by side in sauce. Drizzle remaining sauce over top and down center of shells. Sprinkle with Parmesan cheese and bake, covered, in 350° oven until bubbly.

Serves 6

NUTRITIONAL DATA

PER SERVING		EXCHANGES	
calories	228	milk	0.0
protein (gm)	23.1	vegetable	1.0
fat (gm)	7.4	fruit	0.0
cholesterol (mg)	25	bread	0.5
sodium (mg)	805	meat	3.0
% calories from fat	29	fat	0.0

GREEK PASTA

FETTUCCINE À LA GRECQUE

Vegetable cooking spray

2 teaspoons garlic, minced

2 teaspoons dried oregano

1½ cups Light Tomato Sauce (p. 228), or canned tomato
  sauce

1 teaspoon basil

Pepper, freshly ground

12 ozs. fresh fettuccine

¾ lb. medium shrimp, shelled and deveined

3 ozs. feta cheese, cut into 1-in. chunks

Parsley for garnish

To make Grecque Sauce, spray a skillet with vegetable cooking spray and add garlic and oregano. Cook about 2 minutes. Stir in Light Tomato Sauce and basil and simmer 5 more minutes. Season to taste with pepper.

Put pasta in boiling water and cook until *al dente*.

Meanwhile, spray another skillet with vegetable cooking spray and add shrimp. Sear about a minute on each side. Remove shrimp with slotted spoon. Add the Grecque Sauce to pan and simmer 1–2 minutes. Stir shrimp into sauce and season to taste with pepper. Drop in chunks of feta and basil.

Drain pasta and transfer to pasta bowl. Add shrimp in Grecque Sauce and toss to combine. Sprinkle with parsley. Serve hot.

Serves 4

NUTRITIONAL DATA

PER SERVING		EXCHANGES	
calories	485	milk	0.0
protein (gm)	30.0	vegetable	2.0
fat (gm)	11.3	fruit	0.0
cholesterol (mg)	223	bread	3.5
sodium (mg)	435	meat	2.0
% calories from fat	21	fat	2.0

Note: Grecque Sauce is an all-purpose sauce that can also be used for pizza, steaks, lamb chops, veal, and grilled fish.

MACARONI WITH OLIVE AND TOMATO SAUCE

2 tablespoons olive oil

1 medium red onion, finely chopped

2-3 cups fresh tomato, chopped and peeled

4-5 thin curls of orange rind, grated

1 garlic clove, minced

1-2 cups water

½ cup dry red wine

1 cup Kalamata olives, rinsed, pitted, and sliced

2 scant tablespoons capers, rinsed

3 tablespoons fresh parsley, chopped

1 teaspoon dried thyme

Pepper, freshly ground to taste

1 lb. macaroni

In heavy saucepan, heat olive oil. Add onion and saute until translucent, stirring with wooden spoon. Add tomatoes, orange rind, and garlic. Stir well. Add about 1 cup water, lower heat, and simmer, covered, until sauce thickens, adding more water if necessary. Add wine, uncover pot slightly, and continue simmering about 30 minutes. Add olives and capers and cook for 5 more minutes. Stir in herbs and pepper and cook 10 more minutes.

While sauce is cooking, cook pasta according to package directions. When pasta is cooked, drain well and top with sauce. Serve hot.

Serves 6

NUTRITIONAL DATA

PER SERVING		EXCHANGES	
calories	356	milk	0.0
protein (gm)	11.6	vegetable	1.0
fat (gm)	8.7	fruit	0.0
cholesterol (mg)	65	bread	3.5
sodium (mg)	75	meat	0.0
% calories from fat	22	fat	2.0

SPANISH PASTA

BASQUE SPAGHETTI

1 lb. thin spaghetti

2 tablespoons olive oil

3 large cloves garlic, chopped

20 medium shrimp, peeled and deveined

Pepper to taste

3 tablespoons fresh parsley, minced (divided)

½ cup Parmesan cheese, freshly grated

In large saucepan, bring 3 qts. of water to a boil. Add spaghetti and cook until tender but still firm (8–10 minutes).

Meanwhile, heat olive oil over medium heat in large skillet. Add garlic, cooking until golden; discard garlic pieces. Add shrimp, pepper, and 2 tablespoons parsley to skillet. Cook 1–3 minutes until shrimp turns pink. Remove skillet from heat.

Drain spaghetti and add to skillet. Add Parmesan cheese. Mix and transfer to warmed serving bowl. Sprinkle with parsley; serve.

Serves 6

NUTRITIONAL DATA

PER SERVING		EXCHANGES	
calories	406	milk	0.0
protein (gm)	18.5	vegetable	0.0
fat (gm)	8.8	fruit	0.0
cholesterol (mg)	43	bread	3.5
sodium (mg)	193	meat	2.0
% calories from fat	20	fat	1.0

♥

SALMON LASAGNA IN WHITE WINE SAUCE

This dish is extremely delicate, the blend of flavors enhanced by a light sauce. You will need a 5-cup rectangular terrine; I use a 3x10-in. lidded terrine. You can also use a 9x5-in. loaf pan.

PASTA

5–8 lasagna noodles

1 tablespoon oil

SALMON MOUSSE

1 lb. fresh salmon, skinned and boned, cut into chunks (canned salmon may also be used)

2 egg whites

1 teaspoon Spike

½ teaspoon white pepper, freshly ground

1 cup evaporated skim milk

SAUCE

Vegetable cooking spray

2 medium carrots, finely chopped

3 medium stalks celery, finely chopped

1 medium onion, minced

1 bell pepper, finely chopped

1 cup dry white wine

1 teaspoon Spike

½ teaspoon white pepper, freshly ground

½ cup evaporated skim milk

½ cup chicken broth (low sodium)

Pasta: Cook in boiling water with oil, according to package directions. Drain and immediately plunge into cold water. Remove from water and place on clean towels to drain. Using a piece of wax paper as a pattern to fit bottom of terrine, cut pasta sheets to size.

Salmon Mousse: In food processor or blender, puree salmon with egg whites, Spike, and pepper until smooth. With motor running, pour in evaporated skim milk. Stop motor and scrape down sides of bowl. Whirl again. Remove to a bowl.

Prepare the Terrine: Preheat oven to 350°. Spray terrine with vegetable cooking spray. Place piece of pasta on bottom. Spread one-quarter of salmon mousse on top (if you are using 5 or more pasta skins, use less mousse per layer). Continue, alternating layers of pasta and mousse, ending with pasta on top. Cover terrine with lid or foil. Place terrine inside a larger pan filled with boiling water halfway up the terrine. Bake in preheated oven 30 minutes. To unmold, run a knife around the lasagna and turn out onto a board. Cover to keep warm.

Sauce: Spray skillet with vegetable cooking spray and add carrots, celery, onion, and pepper. Cook slowly 20 minutes. Pour in white wine; cook another 10 minutes. Add Spike and white pepper. Transfer to blender or food processor; puree with evaporated skim milk and chicken broth. Strain through fine-mesh strainer into saucepan. Taste for seasoning and heat through.

Assemble the Dish: Cut lasagna into 8 serving pieces. Pour some sauce over, and pass remainder in sauceboat.

Serves 8

NUTRITIONAL DATA

PER SERVING		EXCHANGES	
calories	268	milk	0.5
protein (gm)	15.7	vegetable	2.0
fat (gm)	5.9	fruit	0.0
cholesterol (mg)	51	bread	1.0
sodium (mg)	112	meat	1.0
% calories from fat	20	fat	1.0

♥

MOROCCAN PASTA

☆

VEGETABLE BIRYANI
(Couscous with Vegetables)

Vegetable cooking spray

3 large onions, sliced

6 chili peppers, crushed into paste, or 2 teaspoons cayenne pepper

1 2-in. piece fresh ginger

10 cloves garlic

½ cup dry lentils, presoaked

½ lb. fresh green peas, shelled

½ lb. carrots, chopped

½ lb. green beans, chopped

3 large tomatoes, chopped

6 whole cloves

1 4-in. stick cinnamon

6 cardamom pods, crushed

1 teaspoon turmeric

3 sprigs fresh mint, or ½ teaspoon dried mint leaves, pounded

1 cup water, heated

6 medium potatoes, chopped into chunks

2 cups couscous, cooked

yogurt (low-fat, plain)

Spray large, heavy skillet with vegetable cooking spray and add onions. Cook until golden brown. With slotted spoon, remove about

⅓ of slices and set aside. Add chili paste, ginger, and garlic and fry 5–6 minutes, stirring constantly. Next add lentils, green peas, carrots, and green beans. Reduce heat and cook 15 minutes, adding water, or a bit of oil, if necessary. Add tomatoes, spices, and mint and stir for 5 minutes. Add about a cup of heated water, cover, and simmer until vegetables are about half-cooked (15 minutes). Add potatoes and cover again; cook another 20–30 minutes until potatoes are tender and water is absorbed.

Serve with couscous and garnish with the reserved onion slices. Pass around a bowl of yogurt for sauce.

Serves 6

NUTRITIONAL DATA

PER SERVING		EXCHANGES	
calories	321	milk	0.0
protein (gm)	11.8	vegetable	3.0
fat (gm)	1.0	fruit	0.0
cholesterol (mg)	0	bread	3.5
sodium (mg)	133	meat	0.0
% calories from fat	3	fat	0.0

Pizza

BASIC PIZZA CRUST

1 tablespoon skim milk
1 package dry yeast
1 cup warm water (105°–115°)
3 cups all-purpose flour (divided)
¼ teaspoon salt
1 teaspoon olive oil
   Vegetable cooking spray
1 tablespoon cornmeal

Add milk and yeast to warm water; let stand 5 minutes for yeast to dissolve. Stir in 2¾ cups flour, salt, and oil to form a soft dough.

Turn dough out onto lightly floured surface. Knead until smooth and elastic (about 5 minutes); add enough of remaining flour, 1 tablespoon at a time, to prevent dough from sticking to hands.

Place dough in bowl, coated with cooking spray, turning dough to coat top. Cover dough and let rise in a warm place (85°), free from drafts, 1 hour or until doubled in bulk. Punch dough down, and divide in half.

Roll each half of dough into a 12-in. circle on a lightly floured surface. Place dough on 12-in. pizza pans or baking sheets coated with cooking spray, and sprinkle each with ½ tablespoon cornmeal. Crimp edges of dough with fingers to form a rim. Cover and let rise in a warm place (85°), free from drafts, 30 minutes.

Top and bake according to recipe directions.

Yield: 2 (12-in.) pizza crusts; 1 crust serves 8.

NUTRITIONAL DATA

PER SERVING		EXCHANGES	
calories	91	milk	0.0
protein (gm)	2.7	vegetable	0.0
fat (gm)	0.5	fruit	0.0
cholesterol (mg)	0	bread	1.5
sodium (mg)	34	meat	0.0
% calories from fat	5	fat	0.0

♥

Note: Store half of dough in freezer up to 1 month if desired. After dough rises first time, punch down and divide in half. Dust half with flour; wrap in plastic wrap; and store in a zip-top, heavy-duty plastic bag in freezer. To thaw, place dough in refrigerator 12 hours or overnight; bring to room temperature and shape as desired.

WHOLE-WHEAT PIZZA CRUST

1 tablespoon sugar
1 package dry yeast
1 cup warm water (105°–115°)
2 cups whole-wheat flour (divided)
1 cup all-purpose flour
¼ teaspoon olive oil
  Vegetable cooking spray
1 tablespoon cornmeal

Dissolve sugar and yeast in warm water in large bowl; let stand 5 minutes. Stir in 1¾ cups flour and next 3 ingredients to form a soft dough. Turn dough out onto lightly floured surface. Knead until smooth and elastic (about 5 minutes); add enough of remaining flour, 1 tablespoon at a time, to prevent dough from sticking to hands.

Place dough in bowl coated with cooking spray, turning to coat top. Cover dough and let rise in a warm place (85°), free from drafts, 1 hour or until doubled in bulk. Punch dough down; divide in half.

Roll each half into a 12-in. circle on lightly floured surface. Place dough on 12-in. pizza pans or baking sheets coated with cooking spray, and sprinkle each with ½ tablespoon cornmeal. Crimp edges of dough with fingers to form a rim. Cover and let rise in warm place (85°), free from drafts, 30 minutes.

Top and bake according to recipe directions.

Yield: 2 (12-in.) pizza crusts; 1 crust serves 8.

NUTRITIONAL DATA

PER SERVING		EXCHANGES	
calories	86	milk	0.0
protein (gm)	3.1	vegetable	0.0
fat (gm)	0.4	fruit	0.0
cholesterol (mg)	0	bread	1.0
sodium (mg)	1	meat	0.0
% calories from fat	4	fat	0.0

Note: Store half of dough in freezer up to 1 month if desired. After dough rises first time, punch down and divide in half. Dust half with flour; wrap in plastic wrap; and store in a zip-top, heavy-duty plastic bag in freezer. To thaw, place dough in refrigerator 12 hours or overnight; bring to room temperature and shape as desired.

PROVENÇAL PIZZA

This pizza is wonderful because the crust is quick and yeastless, and it can be made in minutes if you keep a supply of roasted peppers on hand.

WHOLE-WHEAT CRUST

    2 cups whole-wheat pastry flour
    ½ teaspoon salt
    1 teaspoon baking powder
    ½ teaspoon baking soda
    ½ cup plus 2 tablespoons water (more as needed)
    2 tablespoons olive oil
        Vegetable cooking spray

FILLING

    1 clove garlic, minced
    6 cups red onions, thinly sliced

½ cup dry red wine

¼ cup white wine vinegar

2 tablespoons *herbes de Provençe*

4 plum tomatoes, chopped

1 red bell pepper, roasted (see Note) and cut into thin strips

1 yellow bell pepper, roasted and cut into thin strips

10 Niçoise olives

5-6 fresh basil leaves, cut in slivers

Cornmeal

Crust: Mix together flour, salt, baking powder, and baking soda. Add water and work in with your hands; then add oil and work it in (this can be done in an electric mixer or food processor if you prefer). Dough will be stiff and dry.

Spray a 10-in. pie pan, pizza pan, or quiche pan. Roll out dough about ¼ in. thick and line the pan. Since dough is stiff, this will take some elbow grease. Just keep pounding down with the rolling pin and rolling until you get a flat, round dough. Don't worry if it tears; you can easily patch it together. Pinch a border around top edge and refrigerate until ready to use. (Pizza crust can also be frozen up to 1 month at this point. Defrost before continuing.)

Filling: Spray 10-in. skillet with vegetable spray, and add all filling ingredients except olives and basil. Saute about 10 minutes and remove from heat.

Assembly: Arrange filling over crust and decorate with olives and basil.

Preheat oven to 450°. Bake pizza 10–15 minutes or until crust is golden brown.

Serves 6

NUTRITIONAL DATA

PER SERVING		EXCHANGES	
calories	290	milk	0.0
protein (gm)	8.4	vegetable	3.0
fat (gm)	6.9	fruit	0.0
cholesterol (mg)	0	bread	2.0
sodium (mg)	349	meat	0.0
% calories from fat	20	fat	1.5

Note: To roast bell peppers: preheat broiler. Broil peppers on foil-lined baking sheet until skin is black and sides are evenly charred. Cool in paper bag. Rinse peppers while you slip off skins. Remove seeds, stem, and ribs.

PISSALADIERE
(Provençal Onion Pizza)

No Mediterranean cookbook would be complete without a recipe for Provençal onion pie. This recipe is made with a pizza crust instead of a pastry crust because it's lower in fat, and I prefer it anyway.

1 Basic Pizza Crust (p. 180)
1 tablespoon olive oil
4 lbs. (8 large or 12 medium) onions, very thinly sliced
¼ cup red wine
1 teaspoon *herbes de Provençe*
Pepper, freshly ground
6 anchovy fillets, rinsed (see Note)

Heat olive oil in skillet and add onions. Cook, stirring often, until onions are translucent. Add wine and herbs, and cook gently, stirring occasionally, 1–1½ hours until onions are golden brown and beginning to carmelize. Add freshly ground pepper to taste. Onions should not brown or stick to pan. Add water if necessary.

Preheat oven to 500°. Roll out dough, line pizza pan with it, and top with onions. Cut anchovies in half and make designs over the onions. Bake in preheated oven 20 minutes or until crust is browned and crisp. Remove from oven and serve hot, or let cool and serve at room temperature.

Serves 6

NUTRITIONAL DATA

PER SERVING		EXCHANGES	
calories	272	milk	0.0
protein (gm)	8.3	vegetable	4.0
fat (gm)	3.8	fruit	0.0
cholesterol (mg)	3	bread	2.0
sodium (mg)	202	meat	0.0
% calories from fat	12	fat	0.5

Note: You can use black olives in place of anchovies if you prefer.

PIZZA RUSTICA

1 Whole-Wheat Pizza Crust (p. 181)

1 clove garlic, minced

1 tablespoon olive oil

1 10-oz. package spinach, chopped, thawed, and well drained

2 medium tomatoes, peeled, seeded, and chopped

¼ cup snipped fresh basil, or 1 tablespoon dried, crushed basil

Vegetable cooking spray

1 cup part-skim mozzarella cheese, shredded

1 egg white

In medium skillet, cook garlic in hot oil 30 seconds. Add spinach. Cook and stir 1 minute only until spinach is wilted and remove from heat. Set aside.

Stir together tomatoes and basil; set aside.

Pat half the dough into bottom of sprayed 10-in. spring-form pan or 12-in. pizza pan. Layer in following order, leaving a 1-in. border: ½ cup mozzarella cheese, spinach mixture, tomato-basil mixture, and remaining mozzarella.

On a floured surface, roll remaining dough to a 10-in. or 12-in. circle. Place over filling and seal to bottom crust, pressing filling down lightly and crimping crusts together in decorative manner. Cover and let rise in a warm place 1 hour. Brush with mixture of egg white and 1 tablespoon water. Bake in 375° oven 40 minutes or until done, covering with foil last 10 minutes, if necessary, to prevent overbrowning.

Serves 8

NUTRITIONAL DATA

PER SERVING		EXCHANGES	
calories	190	milk	0.0
protein (gm)	11.7	vegetable	1.0
fat (gm)	6.8	fruit	0.0
cholesterol (mg)	16	bread	1.0
sodium (mg)	170	meat	1.0
% calories from fat	31	fat	1.0

TOMATO, BASIL, AND CHEESE PIZZA

1 Basic Pizza Crust (p. 180)

2 teaspoons olive oil

½ cup fresh Parmesan cheese, grated (divided)

3 large, ripe, unpeeled tomatoes, cut into ¼-in. slices (about 1½ lbs.)

4 cloves garlic, minced

1 teaspoon Spike

1 teaspoon thyme

1 teaspoon tarragon

¼ teaspoon black pepper, freshly ground

½ cup fresh basil, chopped

Brush crust with olive oil. Sprinkle with ¼ cup cheese, leaving a ½-in. border. Arrange tomatoes over cheese, overlapping. Top with garlic, remaining ¼ cup cheese, Spike, thyme, tarragon, pepper, and basil. Bake at 500° for 12 minutes on bottom rack of oven. Remove pizza to cutting board. Let stand 5 minutes.

Serves 6

NUTRITIONAL DATA

PER SERVING		EXCHANGES	
calories	189	milk	0.0
protein (gm)	7.7	vegetable	0.5
fat (gm)	4.9	fruit	0.0
cholesterol (mg)	7	bread	1.5
sodium (mg)	207	meat	0.5
% calories from fat	23	fat	1.0

POTATO-CRUSTED PIZZA

CRUST

1 lb. potatoes, peeled and cut for cooking

1 oz. part-skim mozzarella cheese, shredded

½ tablespoon skim milk

3 egg whites

1 cup all-purpose flour

Vegetable cooking spray

TOPPING

Vegetable cooking spray

3 large cloves garlic, minced

1 teaspoon tarragon

1 teaspoon thyme

6 fresh basil leaves, snipped

1 cup fresh mushrooms, sliced

½ cup fresh Italian parsley, chopped

6 plum tomatoes, peeled and diced

3 tablespoons Romano cheese, freshly grated

Crust: Preheat oven to 400°. Boil potatoes until soft; drain potatoes and mash smooth, free of lumps, adding cheese. Add milk and egg whites, and stir them into potato mixture. Add flour. Spread mixture onto well-sprayed 12-in. metal pizza pan, and bake until crust is lightly browned and a fork inserted in center comes out clean. Perforate entire surface of crust with fork.

Topping: Spray a skillet with vegetable cooking spray and add garlic, tarragon, thyme, basil, and mushrooms. Cook about 2 minutes over medium heat. Remove from heat, and stir in tomatoes and Italian parsley. Place topping on crust. Sprinkle on Romano cheese. Place under broiler about 6 in. from flame. Cook until cheese is bubbly and crust edges are brown. Decorate with dash of chopped parsley, cut into 6 portions, and serve.

Serves 6

NUTRITIONAL DATA

PER SERVING		EXCHANGES	
calories	217	milk	0.0
protein (gm)	9.8	vegetable	1.0
fat (gm)	3.4	fruit	0.0
cholesterol (mg)	10	bread	1.0
sodium (mg)	152	meat	1.0
% calories from fat	14	fat	1.0

PIZZA MARIA

*T*his is a great low-calorie pizza that makes an
excellent lunch, brunch, or late supper.

CRUST

½ cup whole-wheat flour

1 teaspoon dried basil

1 teaspoon dried thyme

3 cloves garlic, minced

8 egg whites

Dash white pepper

1 tablespoon olive oil

FILLING

2 cups fresh tomatoes, diced

½ cup fresh basil, minced, or parsley, chopped

¼ cup mushrooms, chopped

⅓ cup Parmesan cheese, freshly grated

Crust: Preheat oven to 350°. Combine all ingredients for pizza
crust, except olive oil, in mixing bowl. Blend and pour into sprayed
12-in. pizza pan. Bake 15 minutes. Remove from oven and brush
olive oil over surface of pizza crust.

Filling: Add diced tomatoes, basil, mushrooms, and Parmesan
cheese. Bake another 5–10 minutes.

Serves 8

NUTRITIONAL DATA

PER SERVING		EXCHANGES	
calories	90	milk	0.0
protein (gm)	6.8	vegetable	0.5
fat (gm)	3.3	fruit	0.0
cholesterol (mg)	3	bread	0.5
sodium (mg)	139	meat	0.5
% calories from fat	32	fat	0.5

SEAFOOD AND ARTICHOKE PIZZA

½ lb. small fresh shrimp, unpeeled

6 green onions

1 tablespoon plus 1 teaspoon cornstarch

¾ cup evaporated skimmed milk

½ cup part-skim mozzarella cheese, shredded

¼ cup dry white wine

½ teaspoon garlic powder

½ teaspoon pepper, freshly ground

1 Basic Pizza Crust (p. 180)

½ lb. fresh bay scallops

1 14-oz. can artichoke hearts, drained and coarsely chopped

6 fresh basil leaves

2 tablespoons Parmesan cheese, freshly grated

Peel and devein shrimp. Cut each shrimp crosswise into 3 pieces; set aside.

Diagonally slice green onions; set aside.

Combine cornstarch and milk in medium saucepan; stir well. Bring to boil over medium heat, and cook 3 minutes or until thickened, stirring constantly. Remove from heat; stir in mozzarella cheese and next three ingredients.

Spread sauce evenly over prepared pizza crust, leaving a ½-in. border. Arrange shrimp, onions, scallops, artichokes, and basil leaves over sauce. Bake at 500° for 12 minutes on bottom rack of oven. Sprinkle Parmesan cheese over pizza. Bake an additional 7 minutes or until cheese melts. Remove pizza to cutting board and let stand 5 minutes.

Serves 6

NUTRITIONAL DATA

PER SERVING		EXCHANGES	
calories	316	milk	0.5
protein (gm)	27.6	vegetable	1.0

fat (gm)	5.4	fruit	0.0
cholesterol (mg)	89	bread	2.0
sodium (mg)	422	meat	2.0
% calories from fat	15	fat	0.0

PIZZA PRIMAVERA

2 cups fresh broccoli florets

1 cup julienne-cut carrots, 1½-in. long

½ cup fresh snow peas, halved crosswise

½ cup julienne-cut zucchini, 1½-in. long

2 tablespoons cornstarch

1 cup evaporated skimmed milk

¼ cup Parmesan cheese, freshly grated

¼ cup dry white wine

1 teaspoon Spike

½ teaspoon garlic powder

¼ teaspoon black pepper, freshly ground

⅓ cup green onions, sliced

3 tablespoons fresh basil, chopped

½ cup part-skim mozzarella cheese, shredded

1 Basic Pizza Crust (p. 180)

6 cherry tomatoes, cut in half

6 black olives, sliced

Cook broccoli and carrots in boiling water 2 minutes. Add snow peas and zucchini; cook 1 minute. Drain and rinse under cold running water; set aside.

Combine cornstarch and milk in large saucepan; stir well. Bring to boil and cook 2 minutes or until thickened, stirring constantly. Remove from heat; stir in ¼ cup Parmesan cheese and next 4 ingredients. Add broccoli mixture, onion, and basil, tossing gently; set aside.

Sprinkle mozzarella cheese over prepared crust, leaving a ½ in. border. Spoon vegetable mixture on top of cheese. Decorate with tomatoes and olive. Bake at 500° for 12 minutes on bottom rack of oven. Remove pizza to cutting board; let stand 5 minutes.

Serves 6

NUTRITIONAL DATA

PER SERVING		EXCHANGES	
calories	271	milk	0.5
protein (gm)	15.0	vegetable	1.0
fat (gm)	6.0	fruit	0.0
cholesterol (mg)	16	bread	2.0
sodium (mg)	297	meat	1.0
% calories from fat	20	fat	0.5

VEGETARIAN

FRENCH VEGETARIAN

■■

ZUCCHINI STUFFED WITH MUSHROOMS AND CHEESE

This goes well with rice pilaf and salad.

6 medium-size zucchini (6 oz. each)
Vegetable cooking spray
8 shallots, chopped
1 teaspoon thyme
12 large fresh mushrooms
3 cloves garlic, minced
½ cup fresh parsley, chopped
½ cup black olives, sliced
1 tablespoon pimientos, chopped
¼ cup Parmesan cheese, freshly grated

Preheat oven to 300°.

Scrub and trim zucchini; do not peel. Cut lengthwise into halves, and carefully scoop out pulp without damaging shells. You may need to drop zucchini into boiling water for a minute or two if the pulp does not scoop out easily. Drain and plunge into cold water. Drain shells and place them on paper towels to dry.

In large saute pan sprayed with vegetable cooking spray, saute shallots, thyme, mushrooms, garlic, and zucchini pulp about 5 minutes. Put this mixture in large bowl, and add parsley, olives, pimientos, and Parmesan cheese. Toss to mix well.

Fill zucchini shells with the mixture and place them on baking sheet. Bake 10 minutes. Serve immediately.

Serves 6 (2 halves each)

NUTRITIONAL DATA

PER SERVING		EXCHANGES	
calories	71	milk	0.0
protein (gm)	4.7	vegetable	2.0
fat (gm)	3.4	fruit	0.0
cholesterol (mg)	3	bread	0.0
sodium (mg)	138	meat	0.0
% calories from fat	34	fat	0.5

♥

CABBAGE STUFFED WITH VEGETABLES

This is delicious served with green salad and dark bread.

1 medium to large round, green cabbage

Vegetable cooking spray

1 medium-size onion, chopped

2 garlic cloves, minced

2 cups mushrooms, chopped

3 large fresh tomatoes

1 zucchini, chopped

1 15½-oz. can kidney beans

1 teaspoon thyme

1 tablespoon crushed red pepper

3 cups chicken broth (homemade or low sodium)

1 teaspoon basil

1 teaspoon Spike

Pepper, freshly ground

1 bay leaf

Discard any damaged outer leaves from cabbage. Wash cabbage under cold water, then steam or blanch in boiling water 5–7 minutes or until knife goes into center easily. Lift out cabbage and let cool.

Spray skillet with vegetable cooking spray, and saute onion and garlic till onion is translucent. Add mushrooms, tomatoes, zucchini, kidney beans, thyme, and red pepper and cook about 5 minutes.

Place cabbage in large casserole and gently fold back outer leaves to reveal center. Using fruit knife, scoop out center of cabbage to make space for filling. Carefully fold leaves back over filling and tie cabbage together with string. Pour enough chicken stock or water to come halfway up cabbage. Add remaining ingredients and cover casserole. Place in 300° oven 1 hour. Lift out cabbage, remove string, and cut into wedges for serving.

Serves 4

NUTRITIONAL DATA

PER SERVING		EXCHANGES	
calories	184	milk	0.0
protein (gm)	11.4	vegetable	2.5
fat (gm)	2.3	fruit	0.0
cholesterol (mg)	3	bread	1.0
sodium (mg)	424	meat	1.0
% calories from fat	10	fat	0.0

STUFFED PUMPKIN

*T his is always a hit with children for a Hallow-
een party.*

1 4-lb. pumpkin, measuring about 8 in. across
 Vegetable cooking spray
5 cups uncooked sweet potatoes, cut up
½ cup golden raisins
1 teaspoon cinnamon
 Pinch nutmeg
2 Golden Delicious apples, peeled and chopped
3 tablespoons low-calorie pancake syrup

Wash and dry pumpkin. Use short, sharp knife to cut out a lid about 4 in. from top of pumpkin. Scoop out seeds and stringy flesh and discard. Place pumpkin in baking dish sprayed with vegetable cooking spray.

Combine sweet potatoes, raisins, cinnamon, nutmeg, and apples in a bowl. Mix well. Fill pumpkin with mixture and top with syrup. Fit lid back on pumpkin. Bake in 400° oven about 30 minutes until outside of pumpkin is beginning to soften. Lower oven temperature to 300° and continue baking 30 minutes more until flesh is tender. If pumpkin is browning, cover it loosely with foil.

To serve, remove lid and scoop filling and pumpkin into serving dish.

Serves 8

NUTRITIONAL DATA

PER SERVING		EXCHANGES	
calories	289	milk	0.0
protein (gm)	4.3	vegetable	0.0
fat (gm)	0.8	fruit	1.0
cholesterol (mg)	0	bread	3.0
sodium (mg)	28	meat	0.0
% calories from fat	3	fat	0.0

STUFFED EGGPLANT

1 large eggplant
   Vegetable cooking spray
6 shallots, diced
3 cloves garlic, minced
1 lb. porcini or domestic mushrooms, chopped
½ cup chopped celery
1 cup cooked rice
3 plum tomatoes, chopped
6 black olives, sliced
1 cup fresh parsley, chopped
¼ cup Parmesan cheese, freshly grated

Preheat oven to 350°.

Wash eggplant, dry, and place on baking sheet. Bake 10 minutes or until tender. Remove eggplant from oven and slice it down center. Scrape out pulp and set aside. be careful not to damage the half-shells.

Spray a large skillet with vegetable cooking spray and saute the shallots, garlic, mushrooms, celery, and eggplant pulp about 10 minutes. Add rice, tomatoes, olives, and parsley and continue cooking about 5 minutes more. Mix well.

Stuff eggplant shells with the mixture. Top with Parmesan cheese. Bake in shallow baking dish 6–10 minutes. Serve from baking dish immediately.

Serves 4

NUTRITIONAL DATA

PER SERVING		EXCHANGES	
calories	165	milk	0.0
protein (gm)	7.9	vegetable	2.0
fat (gm)	3.8	fruit	0.0
cholesterol (mg)	5	bread	1.0
sodium (mg)	177	meat	0.5
% calories from fat	20	fat	0.5

♥

ITALIAN VEGETARIAN

■

POLENTA WITH MUSHROOMS RAGOUT

This is a very elegant polenta and is very good served with ratatouille. It is also excellent served with a tomato salad and good Italian bread.

>5 cups water, plus additional boiling water in kettle
>
>1 teaspoon Spike
>
>½ lb. (about ½ cups) coarse, stone-ground cornmeal
>
>1 recipe Mushrooms Ragout (recipe follows)
>
>4 tablespoons Parmesan cheese, freshly grated
>
>2 tablespoons fresh parsley, finely chopped, for garnish

Make polenta as follows: Bring 5 cups of water to rolling boil in deep, heavy pot. Have additional water simmering in kettle. Add Spike and reduce heat so water is just boiling, a little above a simmer. Using long-handled wooden spoon, stir water constantly in one direction while you add cornmeal in a stream so slow you can see the individual grains. To do this, hold cornmeal by handfuls and let it run through your fingers. Polenta mixture will become harder and harder to stir as you add all the cornmeal. Never stop stirring. If it seems extremely thick, add boiling water from kettle, a little at a time.

When all cornmeal has been added, continue to stir in same direction 20 minutes. Polenta should come away from sides of pot when done. It may seem done before 20 minutes, but cornmeal won't be cooked properly and won't have creamy consistency of very thick Cream of Wheat; a spoon should stand up in it.

Scrape polenta out of pot onto sprayed cutting board or platter. Make depression in top and pour on Mushrooms Ragout. Sprinkle with Parmesan cheese, garnish, and serve at once.

Serves 8

NUTRITIONAL DATA

PER SERVING		EXCHANGES	
calories	160	milk	0.0
protein (gm)	5.2	vegetable	0.5
fat (gm)	4.0	fruit	0.0
cholesterol (mg)	3	bread	1.5
sodium (mg)	169	meat	0.0
% calories from fat	22	fat	1.0

♥

MUSHROOMS RAGOUT

This is very special when made with wild mush-rooms, but it is also wonderful with cultivated mushrooms.

1 oz. imported dried wild mushrooms, such as cepes, porcini, or chanterelle

Boiling water to cover

Vegetable cooking spray (olive-oil flavored)

2 large shallots, minced

½ lb. fresh wild mushrooms, stems trimmed, thickly sliced

½ lb. fresh cultivated mushrooms (use 1 lb. cultivated mushrooms if fresh wild mushrooms are unavailable), stems trimmed, thickly sliced

4 garlic cloves, minced

½ cup dry red wine

1 cup soaking liquid from dried mushrooms

1 teaspoon thyme

1 teaspoon tarragon

½ teaspoon rosemary

1 cup vegetable stock

Spike and freshly ground pepper

Place dried mushrooms in bowl and pour on boiling water to cover. Let sit 30 minutes while you prepare remaining ingredients.

Spray large skillet with vegetable cooking spray and add shallots. Cook over low heat, stirring often, about 15 minutes or until golden brown. Add fresh wild and cultivated mushrooms or just cultivated mushrooms if wild are not available. Saute 5–10 minutes.

Drain dried mushrooms and retain liquid. Rinse mushrooms thoroughly to remove any debris, squeeze dry, and add to skillet along with garlic and wine. Stir together and saute a few minutes.

Strain soaking liquid from dried mushrooms and measure about 1 cup; add to mushrooms along with thyme, tarragon, rosemary, and vegetable stock. Bring to simmer and simmer, covered, 20 minutes. Uncover and raise heat to high. Reduce liquid by half, and add Spike and pepper to taste.

The ragout will keep a few days and can be frozen.

Serves 8

NUTRITIONAL DATA

PER SERVING		EXCHANGES	
calories	42	milk	0.0
protein (gm)	1.5	vegetable	1.0
fat (gm)	2.0	fruit	0.0
cholesterol (mg)	0	bread	0.0
sodium (mg)	101	meat	0.0
% calories from fat	40	fat	0.5

■

VEGETABLE LASAGNA

*T*his *is a good party recipe because it can be prepared a day or two in advance and refrigerated.*

Vegetable cooking spray

1 small onion, chopped

3 cloves garlic, minced

1 carrot, chopped

1 stalk celery, chopped

2 cups mushrooms, chopped

1 16-oz. can chunky tomatoes, low sodium

1 8-oz. can low-sodium tomato paste mixed with 1 cup water

1 teaspoon oregano

1 teaspoon basil

Spike and freshly ground black pepper

3 cups small broccoli florets

9 lasagna noodles

1 cup low-fat cottage cheese

2 cups low-fat mozzarella cheese, about ¾ lb., shredded

⅓ cup Parmesan cheese, freshly grated

Spray large saucepan with vegetable cooking spray, add onion, and cook until tender. Stir in garlic, carrot, celery, and mushrooms and cook, stirring often, 5 minutes. Add tomatoes and stir in tomato paste, oregano, basil, Spike, and pepper. Simmer, uncovered, 10 minutes or until thickened slightly. Stir in broccoli and continue cooking.

In large pot of boiling water, cook noodles until *al dente;* drain and rinse under cold water.

In lightly sprayed 13x9-in. baking dish, arrange 3 noodles evenly over bottom. Spread with one-half vegetable mixture, then half of cottage cheese. Sprinkle with ⅓ of mozzarella cheese. Repeat noodle, vegetable mixture, cottage, and mozzarella cheese layering once. Arrange remaining noodles over top; sprinkle with remaining mozzarella and Parmesan.

Bake in 350° oven 35–45 minutes or until bubbly.

Serves 8

NUTRITIONAL DATA

PER SERVING		EXCHANGES	
calories	158	milk	0.0
protein (gm)	13.4	vegetable	2.0
fat (gm)	2.8	fruit	0.0
cholesterol (mg)	6	bread	0.5
sodium (mg)	374	meat	1.5
% calories from fat	15	fat	0.0

♥

BAKED STUFFED PASTA SHELLS

18 jumbo pasta shells

4 cups packed spinach, washed, trimmed

2 tablespoons olive oil

2 tablespoons celery, diced

3 tablespoons onion, diced

2 tablespoons fresh mushrooms, finely chopped

1 cup low-fat cottage cheese

1 egg

Black pepper, freshly ground

1 teaspoon dried basil

1 teaspoon dried thyme

3 tablespoons flour

½ teaspoon dry mustard

2½ cups skim milk

¼ cup Parmesan cheese, freshly ground

Cook pasta. Drain, rinse with cold water, and drain again.

Cook spinach over high heat until wilted, about 2 minutes. Drain, chop, and place in medium-size bowl.

Heat olive oil in heavy skillet over medium heat. Saute celery and onion 2 minutes, add mushrooms, and cook another 1 minute. Add to spinach, along with cottage cheese, egg, pepper and herbs.

Add flour and dry mustard to milk and heat to boiling, stirring until thickened. Pour sauce into 9x13-in. baking dish.

Spoon spinach mixture into shells, then place each shell into baking dish. Cover dish with foil, and bake at 375° for 15 minutes. Remove cover, sprinkle with cheese, and bake another 10 minutes.

Serves 6

NUTRITIONAL DATA

PER SERVING		EXCHANGES	
calories	419	milk	0.5
protein (gm)	22.6	vegetable	0.0
fat (gm)	9.4	fruit	0.0
cholesterol (mg)	107	bread	3.5
sodium (mg)	337	meat	1.0
% calories from fat	20	fat	1.5

RISOTTO PRIMAVERA

This rice dish can stand alone as a main dish when served with a vegetable or salad.

    4 cups chicken broth (homemade or low sodium)
      Vegetable cooking spray
    2 onions, chopped
    2 celery stalks, chopped
    2 carrots, chopped
    1 cup fresh parsley, chopped
8-10 fresh basil leaves

2 cups arborio rice (or rice of your choice)

8-10 plum tomatoes, diced

3 small zucchini, sliced thin

1 cup peas

¼ cup Parmesan cheese, freshly grated

Bring chicken broth to simmer.

Spray skillet with vegetable cooking spray and saute onions until soft and golden. Stir in celery, carrots, parsley, basil, and rice. Saute about 2 minutes and add ½ cup of simmering broth. Keep liquid simmering and stir continually, scraping bottom and sides of pan, until liquid has been absorbed.

Add tomatoes, zucchini, peas, and another ½ cup of hot broth; stir continually.

Each time rice becomes dry, add another ½ cup broth. You may not need all the liquid before rice is done; if you need a little more, add water. Cook rice until tender, but a little firm to the bite. Total cooking time should about 30–35 minutes.

Sprinkle with Parmesan cheese before serving.

Serves 6

NUTRITIONAL DATA

PER SERVING		EXCHANGES	
calories	354	milk	0.0
protein (gm)	11.8	vegetable	2.5
fat (gm)	3.5	fruit	0.0
cholesterol (mg)	6	bread	3.5
sodium (mg)	178	meat	0.5
% calories from fat	9	fat	0.0

GREEK VEGETARIAN

STUFFED TOMATOES AND GREEN PEPPERS

This is a popular "taverna" dish, where it's served at room temperature.

6 medium-size or large green bell peppers

6 large, firm, ripe tomatoes

1 recipe Rice and Tomato Stuffing (recipe follows)

1 teaspoon olive oil

3 tomatoes, chopped

3 tablespoons tomato paste

4 large garlic cloves, minced or put through press

Spike and freshly ground pepper

Juice of 1 large lemon

2 tablespoons parsley, mint, or cilantro, freshly chopped

Cut tops off peppers and whole tomatoes, about ½ in. from ends. Save ends, which will serve as caps. Scoop out seeds and membranes from peppers and discard. Scoop out tomato pulp, finely chop, and set aside.

Stuff peppers and tomatoes with Rice and Tomato Stuffing. Replace tops.

Brush bottom of a pot large enough to hold stuffed vegetables with olive oil.

Toss together the reserved tomato pulp, chopped tomatoes, tomato paste, and garlic. Add Spike and freshly ground pepper to taste. Place mixture in pot. Place stuffed tomatoes and peppers on top of mixture. Add lemon juice and enough water so that liquid comes about one-quarter of the way up sides of vegetables. Bring to a simmer. Cover and simmer 45 minutes or until stuffing is thoroughly cooked. Remove tomatoes and peppers from pot and place on plate. Remove tops.

Turn up heat and reduce sauce until it is thick and fragrant. Correct seasonings and pour over vegetables. Allow to cool to room temperature or serve hot. Sprinkle with herbs just before serving. These vegetables will keep a day in the refrigerator.

Serves 6

NUTRITIONAL DATA

PER SERVING		EXCHANGES	
calories	151	milk	0.0
protein (gm)	4.5	vegetable	3.0
fat (gm)	1.9	fruit	0.0
cholesterol (mg)	0	bread	1.0
sodium (mg)	90	meat	0.0
% calories from fat	10	fat	0.0

RICE AND TOMATO STUFFING FOR VEGETABLES

½ lb. (2-3) tomatoes, finely chopped

1 onion, finely chopped

2 garlic cloves, minced

2 small hot green chili peppers, minced

½ cup uncooked rice

½ cup parsley, finely chopped

4-6 tablespoons fresh cilantro

Spike and freshly ground pepper

4 tablespoons fresh lemon juice

Combine all ingredients, and stuff vegetables according to recipe directions. Yield is enough for 2 lbs. of vegetables (tomatoes, eggplant, peppers, or zucchini).

Serves 6

NUTRITIONAL DATA

PER SERVING		EXCHANGES	
calories	79	milk	0.0
protein (gm)	1.9	vegetable	0.0
fat (gm)	0.3	fruit	0.0
cholesterol (mg)	0	bread	1.0
sodium (mg)	7	meat	0.0
% calories from fat	3	fat	0.0

FASOULIA
(Stewed Beans with Tomato and Garlic)

You can use either fava beans or giant white beans of the same shape, which the French call soissons. Favas have an outer skin that must be removed after soaking. Don't remove the skins from the white beans or the beans will fall apart when you cook them.

½ lb. (1½ cups) dried giant white or fava beans, washed and picked over

1 qt. water

4 large garlic cloves, minced

1 bay leaf

3 heaping tablespoons tomato paste

1 teaspoon dried oregano

Spike

1 teaspoon thyme

Juice of 1 large lemon

Pepper, freshly ground

2 tablespoons fresh parsley, chopped

1 small onion, chopped

Soak beans overnight in 3 times their volume of water. Drain beans. If using fava beans, remove outer shells.

Combine beans in large saucepan with water, garlic, bay leaf, and tomato paste. Bring to boil. Reduce heat, cover, and simmer 45 minutes. Add oregano, thyme, and Spike and simmer another 15–30 minutes or until beans are tender but not mushy.

Uncover and raise heat. Reduce liquid until beans are bathed in thick tomato puree. Remove from heat. Add lemon juice and freshly ground pepper to taste. Adjust Spike. Allow to cool or serve hot. Serve garnished with chopped fresh parsley and chopped onion.

Serves 4 as side dish.

NUTRITIONAL DATA

PER SERVING		EXCHANGES	
calories	212	milk	0.0
protein (gm)	12.4	vegetable	1.0
fat (gm)	0.9	fruit	0.0
cholesterol (mg)	0	bread	2.5
sodium (mg)	132	meat	0.0
% calories from fat	4	fat	0.0

SPANISH VEGETARIAN

RICE AND BEAN CASSEROLE

You may want to add a little less chili or cayenne if you have young children. Serve with green salad and black bread.

½ cup water
1 large onion, chopped
2 cloves garlic, minced
2 cups mushrooms, sliced
2 sweet green peppers, chopped
¾ cup long-grain rice
3 cups red kidney beans, drained (about 2 16-oz. cans)
1 lb. plum tomatoes, chopped
1 tablespoon chili powder
2 teaspoons cumin
1 teaspoon cilantro
¼ teaspoon cayenne pepper
1 cup low-fat mozzarella cheese, shredded

In large skillet, heat water over medium heat. Add onion, garlic, mushrooms, and green peppers. Simmer, stirring often, until onion is tender, about 10 minutes. Add rice, beans, tomatoes, chili powder, cumin, cilantro, and cayenne. Cover and simmer about 25 minutes or until rice is tender and most of liquid is absorbed.

Transfer to baking dish and sprinkle with cheese. Bake in 350°
oven 15 minutes, or microwave on High (100%) power 1–2 minutes
or until cheese melts.

Serves 6

NUTRITIONAL DATA

PER SERVING		EXCHANGES	
calories	334	milk	0.0
protein (gm)	20.0	vegetable	2.0
fat (gm)	7.1	fruit	0.0
cholesterol (mg)	21	bread	2.0
sodium (mg)	602	meat	2.0
% calories from fat	19	fat	0.5

DINNER SAUCES

FRENCH DINNER SAUCES

MOCK HOLLANDAISE SAUCE

¼ cup plain low-fat yogurt

¼ cup Hellman's Free mayonnaise

2 teaspoons skim milk

¼ teaspoon dry mustard

Dash white pepper

Place all ingredients in blender and process until smooth.
Makes ½ cup.
Serves 4

NUTRITIONAL DATA

PER SERVING		EXCHANGES	
calories	21	milk	0.0
protein (gm)	0.8	vegetable	1.0
fat (gm)	0.2	fruit	0.0
cholesterol (mg)	1	bread	0.0
sodium (mg)	201	meat	0.0
% calories from fat	9	fat	0.0

CONFITURE DE TOMATES

I first made this sauce when I harvested my own ripe, red, juicy tomatoes for the first time. It freezes well, so make plenty in the summer when tomatoes are inexpensive and plentiful.

    Vegetable cooking spray (olive-oil flavored)

    1 large onion, coarsely chopped

    6 garlic cloves, minced

    2 lbs. tomatoes (fresh are best but canned can be used)

    ¼ cup tomato paste

    ½ teaspoon sugar

    8 fresh basil leaves, chopped, or 1 tablespoon dried basil

    Spike and pepper to taste

Spray a skillet with vegetable cooking spray. Saute onion and garlic until limp. Add tomatoes and tomato paste, sugar, Spike, and pepper. Simmer over medium heat, stirring every so often until thick. This will take about 45 minutes.

Serves 4

NUTRITIONAL DATA

PER SERVING		EXCHANGES	
calories	108	milk	0.0
protein (gm)	2.9	vegetable	2.0
fat (gm)	4.2	fruit	0.0
cholesterol (mg)	0	bread	0.0
sodium (mg)	85	meat	0.0
% calories from fat	32	fat	1.0

■

TOMATO COULIS

A coulis is simply a reduced puree or sauce, often made of vegetables or fruit. This coulis can be served hot or cold. Serve the coulis by spooning a puddle of it onto a plate and setting the food in the middle of the pool.

6 lbs. vine-ripened tomatoes (about 12 average)
2 tablespoons white wine
2 cups yellow onions, finely chopped
    Spike and black pepper, freshly ground to taste
8 fresh basil leaves, minced, or 1 tablespoon dried basil
1 cup fresh parsley, chopped

Bring a large saucepan of water to a boil. Drop tomatoes into boiling water one at a time for 10–15 seconds. Remove with slotted spoon and drop into bowl of cold water. Continue until all tomatoes have been scalded, then drain them.

Peel tomatoes and cut horizontally into halves. Use a melon baller to scoop out seeds and liquid inside tomatoes. Coarsely chop tomatoes and reserve.

Heat wine in large kettle. Add onion, cover, and cook over low heat until onions are tender, about 20 minutes. Stir in chopped tomatoes and bring to boil. Season with Spike and freshly ground black pepper. Reduce heat and simmer, uncovered, about 40 minutes or until coulis is somewhat reduced and thickened.

Transfer coulis to food processor fitted with steel blade or blender, and puree. Return coulis to kettle and add basil and parsley. Simmer 5 minutes more, or longer if you would like a thicker puree. Makes about 2 quarts.

Serves 16 (½ cup servings)

NUTRITIONAL DATA

PER SERVING		EXCHANGES	
calories	61	milk	0.0
protein (gm)	1.8	vegetable	2.0

fat (gm)	2.3	fruit	0.0
cholesterol (mg)	0	bread	0.0
sodium (mg)	18	meat	0.0
% calories from fat	30	fat	0.5

PROVENÇAL SAUCE

This sauce is excellent over chicken, veal, or on a rice side dish.

6 medium-size tomatoes

Vegetable cooking spray (olive-oil flavored)

1 garlic clove, minced

1 tablespoon parsley, chopped

½ teaspoon Spike

⅛ teaspoon pepper, freshly ground

3 fresh basil leaves, chopped

Place tomatoes in boiling water for 1 minute. Peel, remove seeds, and chop.

In saucepan sprayed with vegetable cooking spray, add garlic, tomatoes, parsley, Spike, and pepper. Cook gently 30 minutes. Add basil and cook 10 minutes more. Serve hot over meat or rice.

Makes about 1½ cups.

Serves 6

NUTRITIONAL DATA

PER SERVING		EXCHANGES	
calories	25	milk	0.0
protein (gm)	1.1	vegetable	1.0
fat (gm)	0.0	fruit	0.0
cholesterol (mg)	0	bread	0.0
sodium (mg)	11	meat	0.0
% calories from fat	0	fat	0.0

BASIC BROWN SAUCE

2 tablespoons butter buds

2 medium-size carrots, diced

1 medium-size onion, chopped

2 sprigs parsley

Pinch of thyme

1 small bay leaf

2 tablespoons flour

1 cup dry white wine

1½ cups consommé (canned may be used)

1 tablespoon tomato paste

½ teaspoon Spike

¼ teaspoon pepper, freshly ground

Mix one envelope butter buds with ½ cup warm water. Place 2 tablespoons in small saucepan and add carrots, onions, parsley, thyme, and bay leaf. Cook over low heat, stirring constantly, until vegetables are golden brown.

Stir in flour and cook until slightly brown. Stir in wine and consommé. Add tomato paste, Spike, and pepper. Bring to boil. Cover and simmer 30 minutes. Strain.

Makes 2 cups.

Serves 8

NUTRITIONAL DATA

PER SERVING		EXCHANGES	
calories	51	milk	0.0
protein (gm)	1.7	vegetable	2.0
fat (gm)	0.3	fruit	0.0
cholesterol (mg)	0	bread	0.0
sodium (mg)	172	meat	0.0
% calories from fat	6	fat	0.0

LIGHT BÉARNAISE SAUCE

This sauce is excellent over steak, or it can be used for vegetables.

¼ cup chicken or vegetable stock

1 shallot, minced

¼ cup flour, or 2 tablespoons arrowroot

2 cups skim milk

½ cup non-fat dry milk

1 bay leaf

½ teaspoon white pepper

Heat chicken or vegetable stock and shallot over moderate heat in saucepan. Gradually add flour or arrowroot, and blend with wire whisk. Simmer and stir until heated through but not browned.

Remove from heat and add remaining ingredients. Return to heat and cook, stirring occasionally, until thickened.

Makes 2½ cups.

Serves 10 (¼ cup servings)

NUTRITIONAL DATA

PER SERVING		EXCHANGES	
calories	42	milk	0.5
protein (gm)	3.3	vegetable	0.0
fat (gm)	0.2	fruit	0.0
cholesterol (mg)	1	bread	0.0
sodium (mg)	64	meat	0.0
% calories from fat	4	fat	0.0

MOCK CRÈME FRAÎCHE
(Low-Fat Crème Fraîche)

If a recipe calls for cream, this may be substituted. It is not added in the early stages as part of the cooking process, but a minimum amount is floated in at the last moment before serving to add smoothness without over-richness.

1½ cups low-fat cottage cheese
½ cup plain, low-fat yogurt
¼ cup low-fat ricotta cheese

Put all ingredients into food processor and run until everything is perfectly blended and smooth, no more than 7–8 seconds. Transfer mixture to bowl and, using a wire whisk, beat well to add as much air as possible, until mixture is fluffy and light. It should expand to about 2½ cups in 3–4 minutes.

Pour mixture into jars and set in warm place or on hot plate of a yogurt maker to stay at a steady 75° and begin to ferment. This should take about 2 hours. Mixture will thicken and take on a subtle acid flavor.

Makes about 2½ cups, which can be stored in refrigerator up to 2 weeks for use in many recipes.
Serves 6

NUTRITIONAL DATA

PER SERVING		EXCHANGES	
calories	67	milk	0.0
protein (gm)	9.1	vegetable	0.0
fat (gm)	1.7	fruit	0.0
cholesterol (mg)	7	bread	0.0
sodium (mg)	256	meat	1.5
% calories from fat	23	fat	0.0

■

AIOLI

*T*his sauce is one of the glories of Provençal cookery and has been called the "butter of Provençe." It is wonderful with fish, or served as a dip for fresh raw vegetables.

> 1 cup Hellman's Free mayonnaise
> 5 cloves garlic, minced
> 1 teaspoon Spike
> 2 tablespoons lemon juice
> ½ teaspoon dry mustard
> White pepper, freshly ground

Place all ingredients in blender and process until smooth. Serve with fish or vegetables.

Serves 8

NUTRITIONAL DATA

PER SERVING		EXCHANGES	
calories	28	milk	0.0
protein (gm)	0.1	vegetable	1.0
fat (gm)	0.0	fruit	0.0
cholesterol (mg)	0	bread	0.0
sodium (mg)	380	meat	0.0
% calories from fat	0	fat	0.0

♥

ITALIAN DINNER SAUCES

RED CLAM SAUCE

2 cups onions, chopped

2 cups fresh mushrooms, sliced

6 cloves garlic, minced

2 tablespoons olive oil

½ teaspoon Spike

¼ teaspoon black pepper, freshly ground

1 can chunky tomatoes

4 cans (6½ ozs.) minced clams with liquid

In large saucepan, saute onions, mushrooms, and garlic in oil over medium heat about 5 minutes or until onions are translucent. Add remaining ingredients and cook, covered, 45 minutes.

Makes about 8 cups.

Serves 16

NUTRITIONAL DATA

PER SERVING		EXCHANGES	
calories	104	milk	0.0
protein (gm)	12.7	vegetable	0.0
fat (gm)	2.8	fruit	0.0
cholesterol (mg)	31	bread	0.0
sodium (mg)	134	meat	0.0
% calories from fat	24	fat	0.0

♥

MARINARA SAUCE

"**M**ariner" means sailor, but it was the sailors' wives who waited for their husbands to return home that gave this sauce its name. It's fresh and fast because you can make it while your pasta water is boiling.

Vegetable cooking spray (olive-oil flavored)

5 garlic cloves, minced

2 28-oz. cans ready-cut, peeled, low-sodium tomatoes, or 5 lbs. fresh tomatoes, peeled and sliced

1 6-oz. can tomato paste (low sodium)

4 tablespoons sun-dried tomatoes, chopped (optional)

½ cup mushrooms, sliced

10 fresh basil leaves

Pepper

Parmesan cheese, freshly grated

In a deep skillet sprayed with vegetable cooking spray, saute garlic. Add tomatoes, tomato paste, sun-dried tomatoes (if you are using them), and mushrooms. Cook over medium heat 20–30 minutes, stirring occasionally.

Tear basil leaves into small pieces and sprinkle on top after adding sauce to pasta. Finally, add pepper and grated cheese.

Makes about 2 quarts of sauce.

Serves 16

NUTRITIONAL DATA

PER SERVING		EXCHANGES	
calories	25	milk	0.0
protein (gm)	1.1	vegetable	1.0
fat (gm)	0.3	fruit	0.0
cholesterol (mg)	0	bread	0.0
sodium (mg)	15	meat	0.0
% calories from fat	8	fat	0.0

PUTTANESCA SAUCE

"Puttanesca" means harlot in Italian. This sauce is so named because it is quick to make.

Vegetable cooking spray (olive-oil flavored)

2 to 3 garlic cloves, minced

2 lbs. Italian plum tomatoes, drained and put through food mill or coarse sieve

8 black olives, sliced

1 teaspoon capers

1 teaspoon basil

2 tablespoons fresh parsley, chopped

¼ teaspoon hot pepper flakes

Spray large skillet with vegetable cooking spray, and saute garlic until soft but not brown. Add tomatoes, stir, and simmer about 10 minutes. Stir in olives, capers, basil, parsley, and pepper flakes.

Serves 4

NUTRITIONAL DATA

PER SERVING		EXCHANGES	
calories	63	milk	0.0
protein (gm)	2.4	vegetable	2.0
fat (gm)	2.1	fruit	0.0
cholesterol (mg)	0	bread	0.0
sodium (mg)	59	meat	0.0
% calories from fat	25	fat	0.0

PESTO SAUCE

8 cloves garlic

3 cups fresh basil leaves, tightly packed

1 cup parsley, chopped

⅔ cup Parmesan cheese, freshly grated

¾ cup water

¼ cup white wine vinegar

3 teaspoons capers

2 teaspoons Dijon mustard

Position knife blade in food processor (see Note). Drop in garlic and process 5 seconds or until minced. Add basil and parsley; process 10 seconds or until minced. Add cheese; process until blended. Slowly add remaining ingredients through food chute, with processor running, blending until smooth.

Serves 4 (¼ cup per serving)

NUTRITIONAL DATA

PER SERVING		EXCHANGES	
calories	45	milk	0.0
protein (gm)	3.3	vegetable	1.0
fat (gm)	1.7	fruit	0.0
cholesterol (mg)	4	bread	0.0
sodium (mg)	131	meat	0.0
% calories from fat	30	fat	0.0

Note: A blender can also be used, but add ¼ cup of the water along with the basil and parsley. Add remaining water slowly at end of blending.

GARLIC AND PEPPERS SAUCE

Vegetable cooking spray (olive-oil flavored)

3 garlic cloves, minced

½ cup white wine

2 red bell peppers, coarsely chopped

2 yellow bell peppers, coarsely chopped

1 green bell pepper, coarsely chopped

1 cup fresh mushrooms, sliced

2 tablespoons fresh parsley, chopped

6 basil leaves, coarsely torn

Black pepper, freshly ground

Parmesan cheese, freshly grated

Spray small saucepan with vegetable cooking spray and place over low heat. Saute garlic until soft. Add wine and peppers and cook till peppers are tender, about 8 minutes. Add mushrooms and continue to cook 5 more minutes. Add parsley, basil, and black pepper and cook 5 more minutes. Pour sauce over 1 lb. cooked pasta and sprinkle with cheese.

Serves 4

NUTRITIONAL DATA

PER SERVING		EXCHANGES	
calories	36	milk	0.0
protein (gm)	1.4	vegetable	1.5
fat (gm)	0.0	fruit	0.0
cholesterol (mg)	0	bread	0.0
sodium (mg)	4	meat	0.0
% calories from fat	0	fat	0.0

■|

WHITE CLAM SAUCE

¼ cup olive oil

8 garlic cloves, minced

2 8-oz. bottles clam juice

Juice of 1 lemon

1 cup dry white wine

1 tablespoon oregano

4 tablespoons fresh parsley, minced

1 cup fresh mushrooms, sliced

4 leaves fresh basil, coarsely chopped

6 6-oz. cans minced clams, or 1 36-oz. can

1½ lbs. linguine, or angel hair

Heat oil and saute garlic to golden brown. Add clam juice, lemon juice, wine, oregano, and parsley; heat thoroughly about 20 minutes. Add mushrooms and simmer about 5 minutes. Add basil and clams to the hot clam juice mixture just before you drain your pasta.

Drain pasta and place in hot serving bowl, along with clam sauce. Serves 8

NUTRITIONAL DATA

PER SERVING		EXCHANGES	
calories	617	milk	0.0
protein (gm)	44.3	vegetable	2.0
fat (gm)	10.7	fruit	0.0
cholesterol (mg)	85	bread	4.0
sodium (mg)	393	meat	4.0
% calories from fat	16	fat	1.0

♥

SALSA CRUDA

*T*his uncooked tomato sauce is light and vi-
brant, which makes it a refreshing topping for
bruschetta or poached fish.

2 lbs. firm, ripe tomatoes, peeled, seeded, and chopped
2-3 garlic cloves, minced
10 fresh basil leaves
2 teaspoons balsamic vinegar
Pepper, freshly ground
2 small hot chili peppers, minced

Combine all ingredients. Let stand at room temperature or
refrigerate for later use.
Makes about 2 cups.
Serves 4

NUTRITIONAL DATA

PER SERVING		EXCHANGES	
calories	52	milk	0.0
protein (gm)	2.1	vegetable	2.0
fat (gm)	0.8	fruit	0.0
cholesterol (mg)	0	bread	0.0
sodium (mg)	21	meat	0.0
% calories from fat	11	fat	0.0

LIGHT TOMATO SAUCE

1 tablespoon olive oil

1 tablespoon garlic, minced

½ cup onions, chopped

½ cup mushrooms, sliced

½ cup celery, chopped

2 lbs. Italian tomatoes, undrained

3 fresh basil leaves, chopped

1 tablespoon fresh oregano, chopped

1 teaspoon Spike

Black pepper, freshly ground

Heat oil in heavy, 1½ qt. saucepan over moderate heat. Add garlic, onions, mushrooms, and celery. Saute 5 minutes, stirring well. Add tomatoes, basil, and oregano and bring mixture to simmer. Lower heat, cover, and simmer sauce 1 hour. Season to taste with Spike and pepper.

Makes 3 cups.

Serves 8

NUTRITIONAL DATA

PER SERVING		EXCHANGES	
calories	45	milk	0.0
protein (gm)	1.2	vegetable	1.0
fat (gm)	2.1	fruit	0.0
cholesterol (mg)	0	bread	0.0
sodium (mg)	17	meat	0.0
% calories from fat	38	fat	0.5

Note: You can make this a meat sauce by adding 1 lb. of cooked ground beef or ground turkey.

ROMESCO SAUCE

1 ripe tomato, peeled, seeded, and chopped
1 small, dried hot chili pepper, minced
3 cloves garlic, minced
¾ cup white wine
2 tablespoons wine vinegar
2 tablespoons sherry
1 teaspoon Spike
Black pepper, freshly ground

Pound tomatoes, chili pepper, and garlic to a smooth paste with mortar and pestle. Combine wine, vinegar, and sherry. Add liquid mixture, drop by drop, into paste, stirring constantly in same direction. Season with Spike and pepper to taste.

Makes about 1 cup sauce.

Serves 8

NUTRITIONAL DATA

PER SERVING		EXCHANGES	
calories	24	milk	0.0
protein (gm)	0.2	vegetable	1.0
fat (gm)	0.1	fruit	0.0
cholesterol (mg)	0	bread	0.0
sodium (mg)	3	meat	0.0
% calories from fat	2	fat	0.0

GREEK DINNER SAUCES

AVGOLEMONO SAUCE

Egg substitute equal to 3 eggs
Juice of 1 lemon
1 cup hot chicken broth

Beat egg substitute until frothy. Slowly add lemon juice, beating constantly. Add hot broth, drop by drop, and then a little more at a time, beating constantly. Pour over dish you are serving.

Serves 6

NUTRITIONAL DATA

PER SERVING		EXCHANGES	
calories	33	milk	0.0
protein (gm)	4.7	vegetable	0.0
fat (gm)	1.2	fruit	0.0
cholesterol (mg)	0	bread	0.0
sodium (mg)	186	meat	0.5
% calories from fat	36	fat	0.0

THICK AVGOLEMONO SAUCE

Egg substitute equal to 3 eggs
2 tablespoons flour
2 cups hot chicken broth
Juice of 1 lemon

In saucepan, beat egg substitute; then beat in flour, little by little. Pour in hot broth, drop by drop, stirring well. Cook and stir over low heat until sauce thickens. Do not let it boil. Remove from heat. Add lemon juice. Pour over dish you are serving.

Serves 6

NUTRITIONAL DATA

PER SERVING		EXCHANGES	
calories	49	milk	0.0
protein (gm)	5.9	vegetable	0.0
fat (gm)	1.5	fruit	0.0
cholesterol (mg)	0	bread	0.0
sodium (mg)	317	meat	1.0
% calories from fat	29	fat	0.0

MOCK SOUR CREAM

¾ cup plain low-fat yogurt
¼ cup cottage cheese
1 tablespoon lemon juice

Place all ingredients in blender and process until smooth.
Makes 1 cup.
Serves 8

NUTRITIONAL DATA

PER SERVING		EXCHANGES	
calories	20	milk	0.0
protein (gm)	2.1	vegetable	0.0
fat (gm)	0.5	fruit	0.0
cholesterol (mg)	2	bread	0.0
sodium (mg)	44	meat	0.0
% calories from fat	21	fat	0.0

♥

LEMON HERB SAUCE

T his sauce is wonderful on veal, chicken, pasta, or with vegetables.

Vegetable cooking spray (olive-oil flavored)

1 teaspoon Italian herb seasoning

Juice of 2 lemons

½ cup white wine plus 2 tablespoons

2 cloves garlic, minced

½ cup fresh parsley, chopped

Black pepper, freshly ground

Spray small saucepan with vegetable cooking spray. Add all ingredients, and cook over medium heat until all are heated through (about 15 minutes).

Serves 4

NUTRITIONAL DATA

PER SERVING		EXCHANGES	
calories	25	milk	0.0
protein (gm)	0.3	vegetable	1.0
fat (gm)	0.0	fruit	0.0
cholesterol (mg)	0	bread	0.0
sodium (mg)	5	meat	0.0
% calories from fat	0	fat	0.0

SPANISH DINNER SAUCES

LISBON SAUCE

*S*erve this sauce with fish and meat dishes.

Vegetable cooking spray (olive-oil flavored)
1 small onion, finely chopped
½ cup mushrooms, chopped
½ cup white wine
3 tablespoons flour
1 cup beef broth
1 tablespoon tomato puree
1 tablespoon parsley, chopped
½ teaspoon Spike
Black pepper, freshly ground

Spray saucepan with vegetable cooking spray. Add onion and mushrooms, and cook over moderate heat 3 minutes. Add wine and simmer 10 minutes until wine has reduced slightly. Stir in flour and add beef broth gradually. Stir with whisk to form smooth sauce. Stir in tomato puree and parsley. Season with Spike and pepper.

Makes 1½ cups.

Serves 6

NUTRITIONAL DATA

PER SERVING		EXCHANGES	
calories	34	milk	0.0
protein (gm)	1.7	vegetable	1.5
fat (gm)	0.0	fruit	0.0
cholesterol (mg)	0	bread	0.0
sodium (mg)	143	meat	0.0
% calories from fat	0	fat	0.0

OLIVE SALSA

*T*his sauce can be used over shellfish, fish, chicken, or veal.

6 medium, ripe tomatoes
4 black olives, sliced
2 teaspoons parsley, chopped
2 tablespoons red onion, chopped
¼ cup lemon juice
¼ cup balsamic vinegar
¼ cup white wine
1 teaspoon oregano
2 tablespoons fresh basil, coarsely chopped
Spike
Black pepper, freshly ground

Chop tomatoes into ½-in. chunks. Combine with remaining ingredients except lemon juice, vinegar, and wine. Let stand 30 minutes. Pour off any liquid that has accumulated from the salsa; add lemon juice, vinegar, and wine. Adjust seasonings with Spike and pepper.

Makes about 1¼ cups.

Serves 6

NUTRITIONAL DATA

PER SERVING		EXCHANGES	
calories	46	milk	0.0
protein (gm)	1.2	vegetable	1.0
fat (gm)	1.3	fruit	0.0
cholesterol (mg)	0	bread	0.0
sodium (mg)	38	meat	0.0
% calories from fat	22	fat	0.5

MOROCCAN DINNER SAUCE

☆

HARISSA

Harissa is a fiery condiment based on hot red peppers, olive oil, and garlic. It is used for saffron-flavored fish, soups, and stews. I like it to flavor couscous. A good harissa should be thick, with the consistency of a light mayonnaise. Serve it in a little side dish with a very small spoon.

2 cups dried hot red chili peppers
6 cloves garlic, peeled
1 teaspoon coarse salt (divided)
6 tablespoons coriander seeds
4 tablespoons cumin seeds
1 tablespoon olive oil
10 tablespoons white wine (divided)

Pound garlic cloves in mortar with half the salt until smooth. Remove from mortar and reserve.

Add drained chili peppers to mortar and pound to smooth paste with remaining coarse salt. Remove and add to pounded garlic.

Combine coriander and cumin seeds in mortar and pound until powdered. Return pounded garlic and chili peppers to mortar and add olive oil and 4 tablespoons wine. Pound until smooth. Continue this process, adding in remaining wine, until sauce is smooth and well blended. It will keep indefinitely in sealed jar in refrigerator.

Serves 10

NUTRITIONAL DATA

PER SERVING		EXCHANGES	
calories	129	milk	0.0
protein (gm)	1.5	vegetable	1.0
fat (gm)	12.0	fruit	0.0
cholesterol (mg)	0	bread	0.0
sodium (mg)	221	meat	0.0
% calories from fat	77	fat	1.5

SWEET SAUCES

FRENCH SWEET SAUCES

■

APRICOT SAUCE

This sauce is wonderful over puddings and is the final touch for authentic French apple-sauce (see p. 258).

1½ cups fruit-only apricot jam

½ cup water

2 tablespoons sugar (optional)

1 tablespoon apricot brandy

In saucepan, heat apricot jam and gradually stir in water and sugar. Heat to boiling point, then cook over low heat 5–10 minutes, stirring constantly. Strain. Stir in brandy. Serve hot or cold.

Store in covered jar in a cold place. Before covering, top with 1 or 2 tablespoons apricot brandy.

Makes 1¾ cups.

Serves 7

NUTRITIONAL DATA

PER SERVING		EXCHANGES	
calories	195	milk	0.0
protein (gm)	0.0	vegetable	0.0
fat (gm)	0.0	fruit	3.5
cholesterol (mg)	0	bread	0.0
sodium (mg)	7	meat	0.0
% calories from fat	0	fat	0.0

♥

CHOCOLATE SAUCE

Sometimes only chocolate will do, and cocoa gives you the great taste of chocolate without the fat. Serve this with fresh fruit or over cake or frozen yogurt.

⅓ cup Dutch-processed cocoa, such as Droste or Lindt

¼ cup light brown sugar, firmly packed

½ cup buttermilk

2 teaspoons Crème de Cacao, or Kahlua

Combine cocoa and brown sugar in small saucepan. Gradually add buttermilk, stirring with a whisk to blend well. Place pan over medium heat, and continue stirring until sugar dissolves, about 3 minutes. Remove from heat and stir in liqueur. The sauce will thicken as it cools. Keeps in refrigerator several weeks in a tightly closed container.

Makes ¾ cup.

Serves 12 (1-tablespoon servings)

NUTRITIONAL DATA

PER SERVING		EXCHANGES	
calories	31	milk	0.0
protein (gm)	1.0	vegetable	0.0
fat (gm)	0.4	fruit	0.5
cholesterol (mg)	0	bread	0.0
sodium (mg)	13	meat	0.0
% calories from fat	13	fat	0.0

RASPBERRY COULIS

A coulis is simply a reduced puree or sauce, often made of fruit or vegetables. Spoon this elegant sauce over fresh fruit or frozen yogurt.

2 10-oz. boxes frozen raspberries, thawed

⅔ cup sugar, or 8 packets Equal®

2 tablespoons Cointreau

8 whole berries for garnish (optional)

Drain berries of syrup, which may be reserved for another use such as a drink or gelatin dessert. Puree berries in food processor or blender, push through sieve, then return the puree to blender or processor. Add sugar or Equal®, and process until sweetener has dissolved. Add Cointreau.

Serves 8 (2-tablespoon servings)

NUTRITIONAL DATA

PER SERVING		EXCHANGES	
calories	142	milk	0.0
protein (gm)	0.5	vegetable	0.0
fat (gm)	0.1	fruit	2.5
cholesterol (mg)	0	bread	0.0
sodium (mg)	0	meat	0.0
% calories from fat	1	fat	0.0

♥

Note: Strawberries can be used in place of raspberries.

PEAR SAUCE

4 cups ripe pears (about 1½ lbs.), peeled and cubed
2 tablespoons water
3 tablespoons brown sugar, or 6 packets Equal®
⅛ teaspoon ground crystallized ginger

Combine pears and water in medium saucepan; cook, covered, over low heat 45 minutes or until tender. Stir in brown sugar* and ginger; partially mash until chunky. Cook over low heat 5 minutes, stirring frequently. Serve warm or chilled.

You can store pear sauce in refrigerator in an airtight container up to 1 week.

Makes 2½ cups.

Serves 6

NUTRITIONAL DATA

PER SERVING (using sugar)		EXCHANGES	
calories	93	milk	0.0
protein (gm)	0.4	vegetable	0.0
fat (gm)	0.4	fruit	1.5
cholesterol (mg)	0	bread	0.0
sodium (mg)	2	meat	0.0
% calories from fat	4	fat	0.0

♥

*Note: If using Equal®, add after cooking.

ITALIAN SWEET SAUCES

ORANGE SAUCE

3 tablespoons cornstarch
Dash salt
1⅓ cups hot water
3 packets Equal®
4 teaspoons diet margarine
½ cup quick-frozen concentrated orange juice

Combine cornstarch and salt in saucepan. Add hot water gradually, stirring constantly. Cook and stir over medium heat until thick and somewhat clear, about 5 minutes. Remove from heat and stir in Equal® and margarine. Blend in concentrated orange juice. Blend till smooth.

Makes 2 cups.

Serves 16 (2-tablespoon servings)

NUTRITIONAL DATA

PER SERVING		EXCHANGES	
calories	22	milk	0.0
		vegetable	0.0
		fruit	0.0
		bread	0.0
		meat	0.0
		fat	0.0

COFFEE SAUCE

Egg substitute equal to 2 eggs
½ cup strong boiling coffee
¼ cup sugar, or 6 packets Equal®
½ cup evaporated skim milk

Beat egg substitute. Slowly beat in coffee and add sugar*. Cook over but not in boiling water, and stir sauce in top of double boiler with a spoon. Chill. Shortly before serving, fold in evaporated skim milk.

Makes about 1½ cups.

Serves 6

NUTRITIONAL DATA

PER SERVING (using sugar)		EXCHANGES	
calories	65	milk	1.0
protein (gm)	4.1	vegetable	0.0
fat (gm)	0.7	fruit	0.0
cholesterol (mg)	1	bread	0.0
sodium (mg)	62	meat	0.0
% calories from fat	10	fat	0.0

♥

*Note: If using Equal®, add after cooking.

GREEK SWEET SAUCE

ORANGE YOGURT SAUCE

This is wonderful over fresh fruit.

1 cup plain yogurt

1 teaspoon orange rind, grated

2 tablespoons brown sugar, or 2 packets Equal®

½ teaspoon orange extract

Mix all ingredients together.
Makes about 1 cup.
Serves 6

NUTRITIONAL DATA

PER SERVING		EXCHANGES	
calories	42	milk	0.5
protein (gm)	2.0	vegetable	0.0
fat (gm)	0.6	fruit	0.0
cholesterol (mg)	2	bread	0.0
sodium (mg)	28	meat	0.0
% calories from fat	13	fat	0.0

♥

SPANISH SWEET SAUCE

LEMON RUM SAUCE

1 tablespoon lemon rind

2 tablespoons lemon juice

2 tablespoons granulated sugar, or 2 packets Equal®*

3 tablespoons fruit-only orange marmalade

¼ cup water

2 tablespoons rum, or 2 teaspoons rum extract

Orange peel strips for garnish

In saucepan, mix together lemon rind, lemon juice, sugar*, marmalade, and water and bring mixture to boil. Boil 1 minute. Remove from heat, add rum, and transfer to serving dish. Garnish with orange peel.

Serves 4

NUTRITIONAL DATA

PER SERVING (using sugar)		EXCHANGES	
calories	79	milk	0.0
protein (gm)	0.0	vegetable	0.0
fat (gm)	0.0	fruit	1.0
cholesterol (mg)	0	bread	0.0
sodium (mg)	2	meat	0.0
% calories from fat	0	fat	0.0

*Note: If using Equal®, add after cooking.

MOROCCAN SWEET SAUCES

STRAWBERRY-PINEAPPLE SAUCE

This sauce is especially good over frozen vanilla or strawberry yogurt or over pineapple sherbet.

1 8-oz. jar fruit-only strawberry jam

1 8-oz. jar fruit-only pineapple jam

¼ cup sweet wine or brandy

Combine jams and thin to sauce consistency with wine or brandy. Makes about 2 cups.
Serves 10

NUTRITIONAL DATA

PER SERVING		EXCHANGES	
calories	180	milk	0.0
protein (gm)	0.0	vegetable	0.0
fat (gm)	0.0	fruit	3.0
cholesterol (mg)	0	bread	0.0
sodium (mg)	7	meat	0.0
% calories from fat	0	fat	0.0

CHEESE SAUCE

½ cup non-fat buttermilk

2 tablespoons Parmesan or Romano cheese, grated

1 teaspoon cornstarch

½ teaspoon Dijon mustard

Combine milk and other ingredients in small saucepan; mix well. Bring to boil, stirring constantly. Reduce heat to low and cook 2 minutes or until thickened, stirring constantly. Remove from heat.
    Serves 8

NUTRITIONAL DATA

PER SERVING		EXCHANGES	
calories	14	milk	0.0
protein (gm)	1.1	vegetable	0.0
fat (gm)	0.5	fruit	0.0
cholesterol (mg)	1	bread	0.0
sodium (mg)	48	meat	0.0
% calories from fat	33	fat	0.0

BOURBON SAUCE
(or Vanilla Sauce*)

1 cup skim milk

¼ cup egg substitute

3 tablespoons sugar

3 tablespoons bourbon, or to taste

Heat milk in saucepan until hot. Whisk together egg substitute and sugar in small bowl. Whisk hot milk into sugar mixture and pour back into pan. Cook over medium heat, stirring constantly, until thickened, about 5 minutes. Remove from heat and whisk in bourbon.

Serves 12

NUTRITIONAL DATA

PER SERVING		EXCHANGES	
calories	33	milk	0.0
protein (gm)	1.3	vegetable	0.0
fat (gm)	0.2	fruit	0.0
cholesterol (mg)	0	bread	0.5
sodium (mg)	20	meat	0.0
% calories from fat	7	fat	0.0

*For **Vanilla Sauce,** prepare as above but replace bourbon with vanilla.

DESSERTS

FRENCH DESSERTS

■

CHERRY CLAFOUTI

A *"clafouti" is a sort of cross between a flan and a fruit-filled pancake. June is cherry season in Provençe, and August is cherry season in Door County, Wisconsin. In either locale, this is a dessert perfect for cherries.*

Vegetable cooking spray
1 lb. black cherries
¼ cup skim milk
4 tablespoons mild-flavored honey
3 egg whites
1 egg yolk
1 tablespoon vanilla extract
Pinch salt
½ cup unbleached white flour, sifted

Preheat oven to 350°. Spray a 10-in. baking dish.

Pit cherries and place them in bowl; strain off any juices from pits; retain juice.

In a blender or food processor, blend together milk, honey, juice from pitted cherries, eggs, vanilla, and salt. Add flour and continue to blend together 1 more minute, until completely smooth.

Pour batter into bowl containing cherries, mix well, and turn into the sprayed baking dish. Bake 45 minutes to 1 hour, until clafouti puffed and browned and a knife comes out clean when inserted in center. Serve hot or warm. The clafouti will fall a bit upon cooling.

Serves 8

NUTRITIONAL DATA

PER SERVING		EXCHANGES	
calories	121	milk	0.0
protein (gm)	4.3	vegetable	0.0
fat (gm)	0.9	fruit	1.0
cholesterol (mg)	27	bread	0.0
sodium (mg)	77	meat	1.0
% calories from fat	7	fat	0.0

♥

CHOCOLATE MADELEINES*

*T*his is a traditional French cookie you can serve
with frozen yogurt or just with coffee.

3 ozs. unsweetened chocolate

2 ozs. semisweet chocolate

3 tablespoons skim milk

1 cup whole-wheat flour

1 cup unbleached flour

2 teaspoons baking soda

1½ cups espresso

¼ cup apple juice

2 tablespoons unsalted butter

½ cup sugar

1 whole egg plus 2 whites

Vegetable cooking spray

Preheat oven to 350°.

Put the two chocolates and milk in double boiler and cook over low heat until chocolate is melted, about 5 minutes. Remove from heat and set aside to cool slightly.

Blend flour and baking soda together and set aside.

Combine espresso and apple juice in a separate bowl.

Cream butter and sugar together in a mixer. Add eggs and mix well. Add melted chocolate. Alternately add the flour and espresso mixtures. Mix until all ingredients are blended.

Spray a madeleine pan with vegetable cooking spray and fill each scallop three-quarters full. Bake 10–15 minutes. Leave madeleines in pan until completely cooled, then transfer to airtight containers for storing.

Makes 30 madeleines.

Serves 15

NUTRITIONAL DATA

PER SERVING		EXCHANGES	
calories	152	milk	0.0
protein (gm)	3.8	vegetable	0.0
fat (gm)	6.4	fruit	0.0
cholesterol (mg)	19	bread	1.5
sodium (mg)	124	meat	0.0
% calories from fat	35	fat	1.0

♥

*Note: This recipe is not recommended for people with diabetes because of its high sugar content.

BREAD PUDDING WITH RAISINS

1 envelope unflavored gelatin

2 cups milk

2 eggs slightly beaten

1 teaspoon vanilla

6 packets Equal®

2½ cups white bread cubes (about 4 slices)

¼ cup raisins

¼ teaspoon nutmeg

Soften gelatin in ¼ cup milk. Scald remaining milk in top of double boiler. Add softened gelatin. Stir until gelatin dissolves completely. Pour hot milk slowly over eggs, stirring constantly. Return to double boiler, and cook over hot water until mixture coats a spoon. Remove from heat.

Add vanilla and Equal®. Beat until frothy. Stir in bread cubes and raisins. Pour into 1½-qt. mold that has been rinsed in cold water. Cover and refrigerate.

At serving time, unmold and sprinkle with nutmeg. This dish can also be served with a fruit sauce.

Serves 6

NUTRITIONAL DATA

PER SERVING		EXCHANGES	
calories	130	milk	0.0
		vegetable	0.0
		fruit	1.0
		bread	0.0
		meat	1.0
		fat	0.0

♥

■ □

PAIN D'EPICES*
(Spice Cake)

This cake is especially good with cinnamon-flavored frozen yogurt.

    2 cups flour

    ½ cup granulated sugar

    1 teaspoon baking soda

    1 cup milk

    1 teaspoon anisette

    1 teaspoon rum

    1 teaspoon cinnamon

    1 tablespoon honey

    ½ cup blanched almonds, slivered

In mixing bowl, combine flour, sugar, soda, milk, anisette, rum, and cinnamon. Work with wooden spoon until smooth. Cover and let stand overnight at room temperature. When ready to cook, stir in honey and almonds.

Turn dough into loaf pan 8x5x3 in., sprayed with vegetable cooking spray; fill no more than halfway. Cover with aluminum foil. Bake at 400° for 45 minutes. Unmold while hot. Serve cold, sliced.

Pain d'Epices keeps for quite a while in aluminum foil.

Serves 10

NUTRITIONAL DATA

PER SERVING		EXCHANGES	
calories	178	milk	0.0
protein (gm)	4.6	vegetable	0.0
fat (gm)	3.3	fruit	0.0
cholesterol (mg)	0	bread	2.0
sodium (mg)	96	meat	0.0
% calories from fat	16	fat	0.5

Note: This recipe is not recommended for people with diabetes because of its high sugar content.

PÈCHES MELBA

T his dessert was created by the great French chef, Escoffier, to honor the Australian operatic soprano Nellie Melba.

1 cup sugar, or 12 packets Equal®*

1 cup water

1 teaspoon vanilla extract

3 large, firm peaches

1 pt. fully ripe raspberries

¼ cup sugar

1 qt. vanilla frozen yogurt

In saucepan, combine 1 cup sugar* and water. Place over medium heat and stir constantly until mixture boils. Cover and boil 5 minutes. Remove from heat and stir in vanilla extract. Set aside.

Wash, pare, cut into halves, and pit peaches. Put syrup mixture back over medium heat. Add peaches, two halves at a time, and simmer 3 minutes. Chill in refrigerator.

Meanwhile, wash and process raspberries in blender. Stir in ¼ cup sugar. Chill in refrigerator.

When ready to serve, spoon yogurt into 6 glass dishes. Place one-half peach on each dish and spoon raspberries into center of each peach half. Serve immediately.

Serves 6

NUTRITIONAL DATA

PER SERVING (using sugar)		EXCHANGES	
calories	223	milk	0.0
protein (gm)	5.3	vegetable	0.0
fat (gm)	1.6	fruit	1.0
cholesterol (mg)	0	bread	2.0
sodium (mg)	0	meat	0.0
% calories from fat	6	fat	0.0

*Note:** If using Equal®, boil water alone and remove from heat before adding Equal®. Add vanilla extract and set aside. Proceed as above.

CHERRIES JUBILEE

*C reated by the great Escoffier in honor of Queen
Victoria's Jubilee, this has remained a festive
banquet dessert that can easily be made at home.
It goes perfectly with champagne.*

- 1 1-lb. can Bing cherries
- 2 tablespoons arrowroot, dissolved in 2 tablespoons water
- 1 tablespoon kirsch

Drain cherries. Reserve juice from can. In chafing dish or skillet, heat juice. Bring to boil and cook 10 minutes. Add cherries. Bring again to boil. Add arrowroot and continue boiling a few seconds until liquid thickens. Sprinkle with slightly warmed kirsch and ignite! Serve quickly.

Serves 4

NUTRITIONAL DATA

PER SERVING		EXCHANGES	
calories	135	milk	0.0
protein (gm)	0.8	vegetable	0.0
fat (gm)	0.1	fruit	2.0
cholesterol (mg)	0	bread	0.0
sodium (mg)	8	meat	0.0
% calories from fat	1	fat	0.0

FRENCH APPLESAUCE

8 medium-size (2–3 lbs.) tart cooking apples

3 tablespoons water

¼ cup butter buds

½ teaspoon lemon peel, grated

½ cup sugar, or 12 packets Equal®*

½ cup Apricot Sauce (p. 239)

2 tablespoons water

Wash, quarter, pare, and core apples. Put apples in saucepan with water, butter buds, and grated lemon peel. Cook on medium heat, stirring occasionally. Simmer, covered, 15 minutes or until apples are soft and somewhat transparent. Stir in sugar* and continue cooking over low heat until sugar is dissolved.

You can serve this hot, sprinkled with confectioner's sugar. But to serve applesauce cold in true French style, pour heated Apricot Sauce over cold applesauce before serving.

Serves 6

NUTRITIONAL DATA

PER SERVING (using sugar)		EXCHANGES	
calories	204	milk	0.0
protein (gm)	0.3	vegetable	0.0
fat (gm)	0.7	fruit	3.5
cholesterol (mg)	0	bread	0.0
sodium (mg)	2	meat	0.0
% calories from fat	3	fat	0.0

*Note: If using Equal®, add it after apples are cooked and removed from heat but before adding confectioner's sugar or Apricot Sauce.

■

OEUFS À LA NEIGE*
(Floating Island)

This is an easy-to-make dessert that looks as good as it tastes.

2½ cups skim milk

⅓ cup granulated sugar

½ teaspoon lemon rind, grated

3 egg whites

¼ teaspoon salt

¼ cup powdered sugar

Egg substitute equal to 4 eggs

1 teaspoon cornstarch

8 tablespoons granulated sugar

Scald milk in large skillet. Add granulated sugar and lemon rind. Cover. Take skillet off heat.

In a bowl, beat egg whites with salt until foamy, then gradually beat in powdered sugar, beating until stiff.

Return skillet to heat and bring milk to boil. Lower heat and keep at gentle simmer. With kitchen spoon, lift spoonfuls of beaten egg whites and drop them into milk. Never do more than 4 spoonfuls at a time. Cook 1½ minutes. Turn egg whites and cook other side 2 minutes. Remove with slotted spoon and drain on dry cloth.

Whisk together the egg substitute, cornstarch, and 8 tablespoons sugar in small bowl. Whisk the hot milk into mixture, and then pour back into skillet. Cook over medium heat, stirring constantly, until thickened, about 5 minutes. Remove from heat, and pour mixture into serving bowl. Chill.

When ready to serve, float the cooked egg whites on top of the sauce.

Serves 6

NUTRITIONAL DATA

PER SERVING		EXCHANGES	
calories	102	milk	0.5
protein (gm)	5.2	vegetable	0.0
fat (gm)	0.2	fruit	1.0
cholesterol (mg)	2	bread	0.0
sodium (mg)	169	meat	0.0
% calories from fat	2	fat	0.0

*Note: This recipe is not recommended for people with diabetes because of its high sugar content.

CRÈPES WITH RASPBERRY COULIS

BATTER

> Egg substitute equal to 2 eggs
> ¼ cup skim milk
> 2 tablespoons water
> 4 tablespoons all-purpose flour
> Vegetable cooking spray

COULIS

> 3 cups raspberries, or 2 10-oz. packages frozen, thawed
> ¼ cup sugar, or 6 packets Equal®
> 2 tablespoons Cointreau

Batter: Beat egg substitute, milk, and water. Add flour and beat just until smooth. Spray a crêpe pan with non-stick vegetable spray. Heat pan over medium heat. When pan is hot, spoon 2 tablespoons batter into pan and rotate pan to spread evenly. When edges of crêpe are browned, turn crêpe onto a plate. Makes 12 crêpes.

Coulis: Combine raspberries, sugar or Equal®, and Cointreau. Mix well. Fill each crêpe with raspberries and roll up, jelly-roll style. Top with remaining sauce or dust with confectioner's sugar.
   Serves 6 (2 crêpes per serving)

NUTRITIONAL DATA

PER SERVING		EXCHANGES	
calories	112	milk	0.0
protein (gm)	4.0	vegetable	0.0
fat (gm)	1.1	fruit	1.0
cholesterol (mg)	0	bread	0.5
sodium (mg)	42	meat	0.5
% calories from fat	9	fat	0.0

■

COEUR À LA CRÈME

T his is a traditional French dessert. It is very nice served on Valentine's Day, for a wedding shower, or on any special occasion. It is excellent with strawberries, raspberries, blackberries, blueberries, or peaches.

4 teaspoons unflavored gelatin

¼ cup cold water

1½ cups evaporated skim milk

2 tablespoons sugar

2¼ cups plain, low-fat yogurt

1 teaspoon vanilla

2 cups berries, fresh or frozen, thawed

1 teaspoon lemon juice

2 packets Equal®

In a small bowl, soften gelatin in cold water for about 10 minutes.

In a saucepan, combine skim milk and sugar, then cook over moderate heat, stirring constantly, for 5 minutes or until sugar is dissolved. Remove from heat, add gelatin mixture, and stir until gelatin is dissolved. Transfer to a bowl. Let mixture cool about 5 minutes, then whisk in yogurt and vanilla. Mix well.

Rinse 6 individual coeur à la crème molds, and line them with cheesecloth, leaving some cheesecloth extended over edges. Pour in gelatin-yogurt mixture and chill overnight so yogurt can drain. Remove from refrigerator and unmold by turning the coeur onto a serving plate and removing the cheesecloth.

Sprinkle berries with lemon juice and Equal®, and arrange them around the coeur à la crème.

Serves 6

NUTRITIONAL DATA

PER SERVING		EXCHANGES	
calories	141	milk	1.0
protein (gm)	10.8	vegetable	0.0
fat (gm)	1.6	fruit	1.0

cholesterol (mg)	8	bread	0.0
sodium (mg)	135	meat	0.0
% calories from fat	10	fat	0.0

♥

APPLE TART TATIN

Tarte Tatin is named for two impoverished gentlewomen who were forced to earn their living by baking their father's favorite pie. Needless to say, it sold very well.

CRUST

½ cup whole-wheat pastry flour

½ cup unbleached white flour

¼ teaspoon salt

½ teaspoon baking powder

2 tablespoons unsalted butter, softened

1 tablespoon mild-flavored honey

¼ to ⅓ cup cold water (as needed)

FILLING

2 lbs. Golden Delicious apples, about 6 medium

¼ cup corn-oil margarine

½ cup brown sugar, packed lightly

Crust: Mix together the flours, salt, and baking powder. Cut in butter, either in a food processor or by rubbing flour briskly between the palms of your hands. Add honey, mixing it into flour/butter mixture in food processor or with wooden spoon. Add water, a little at a time, mixing it in until dough comes together in a ball. It should be neither sticky nor dry.

Gently gather dough into a ball, wrap in plastic, and set aside while you prepare filling. The dough can be prepared a day or two ahead of time, wrapped in plastic, and refrigerated until you are ready to roll it out.

Filling: Peel apples and core, using a melon baller. Melt margarine over medium heat in 10-in. skillet. Add brown sugar and stir until mixed. Add apples and stir to coat with sugar mixture. Cover pan and cook over medium heat just until apples can easily be pierced with a fork, about 20 minutes. Do not overcook or apples will become mushy. Remove from heat and cool to room temperature. When apples have cooled, place them in pie pan.
Heat oven to 375°.

Assembly: Remove dough from refrigerator and roll into a circle slightly larger than top of pie pan. Place dough over cooled apples, and carefully tuck it in around the apples. Trim off excess dough. Pierce a few steam holes in crust with fork tines. Bake until crust is golden brown, 25–30 minutes.

To Serve: Turn pan upside down onto serving plate. If any apples stick to bottom of pan, remove, and place them on top of tart.
Serves 6

NUTRITIONAL DATA

PER SERVING		EXCHANGES	
calories	343	milk	0.0
protein (gm)	2.8	vegetable	0.0
fat (gm)	12.5	fruit	1.5
cholesterol (mg)	11	bread	2.0
sodium (mg)	226	meat	0.0
% calories from fat	31	fat	2.0

Fresh Figs Poached in Wine*

2 cups red wine
¼ cup orange juice
2 tablespoons orange zest
6 tablespoons mild-flavored honey
½ teaspoon vanilla extract
1 lb. ripe fresh figs
½–1 cup plain, low-fat yogurt
Mint sprigs (for garnish)

Combine wine, orange juice, zest, honey, and vanilla extract in saucepan and bring to boil.

Make a lengthwise incision in each fig, but do not cut them in half. This will allow each fig to become infused with the sauce.

Bring wine to a simmer and drop in figs. If they are very ripe, turn off heat and let them sit 5–10 minutes. If they are not quite ripe, poach them 15 minutes. Carefully remove figs from wine with slotted spoon and place in flat dish with low sides.

Strain wine and return it to the saucepan. Bring to boil and reduce by about one-third. Pour over figs.

You can allow figs to cool or serve them warm with a dollop of yogurt. Garnish with mint sprigs.

Serves 4

NUTRITIONAL DATA

PER SERVING		EXCHANGES	
calories	292	milk	0.0
protein (gm)	2.7	vegetable	0.0
fat (gm)	0.8	fruit	5.0
cholesterol (mg)	2	bread	0.0
sodium (mg)	29	meat	0.0
% calories from fat	·2	fat	0.0

*Note: This recipe is not recommended for people with diabetes because of its high sugar content.

ITALIAN DESSERTS

PEARS IN RED WINE

4 large, firm, ripe pears
1 cup sweet red wine
½ cup sugar, or 8 packets Equal®*
1 teaspoon orange rind, grated
½ teaspoon lemon rind, grated
¼ teaspoon ground cinnamon
1 clove

Quarter, core, and peel pears. Arrange in an 8-in. baking dish.
Heat together wine, sugar,* orange rind, lemon rind, cinnamon, and clove. Bring to boil; pour over pears. Bake in moderate 350° oven about 30 minutes or until pears are tender. Serve warm with frozen yogurt or chilled with whipped diet topping.
Serves 4

NUTRITIONAL DATA

PER SERVING (using sugar)		EXCHANGES	
calories	230	milk	0.0
protein (gm)	0.8	vegetable	0.0
fat (gm)	0.7	fruit	4.0
cholesterol (mg)	0	bread	0.0
sodium (mg)	3	meat	0.0
% calories from fat	2	fat	0.0

♥

*Note: If using Equal®, add after pears have baked in oven.

MELON WITH CHAMPAGNE

2 cantaloupes

2 cups champagne, or other sparkling wine

4 mint sprigs (for garnish)

Cut each cantaloupe in half and discard seeds. Remove meat with melon ball scoop and replace balls in cantaloupe shells. Pour champagne over each half and chill 30 minutes before serving. Garnish with mint sprig.

Serves 4

NUTRITIONAL DATA

PER SERVING		EXCHANGES	
calories	303	milk	0.0
protein (gm)	5.8	vegetable	0.0
fat (gm)	1.8	fruit	5.0
cholesterol (mg)	0	bread	0.0
sodium (mg)	57	meat	0.0
% calories from fat	5	fat	0.0

■

WAFER CUPS WITH FRESH FRUIT

T his is a great dessert because you can make several batches of wafer cups and freeze them for later use.

⅓ cup sugar

⅓ cup egg whites

2 tablespoons flour

1 tablespoon unsalted butter, melted

2 tablespoons poppy seeds

   Vegetable cooking spray

6 cups fresh or frozen berries or peaches

2 tablespoons lemon juice

4 packets Equal®

Preheat oven to 425°. To make wafer cups, whisk together sugar and egg whites until mixture is smooth. Add flour, blend until smooth, and add melted butter and poppy seeds.

Spray a baking sheet with vegetable cooking spray, and drop tablespoons of batter at widely spaced intervals. Using back of a spoon, spread each cookie to 6-in. diameter. Bake in 425° oven 8–10 minutes until golden.

Remove from oven and gently press into small custard cups to mold. Allow to dry, unmold, and store in airtight container in a cool, dry place. Wafer cups will keep for about 1 month. Makes 12 wafer cups.

To make filling for wafer cups, place berries, lemon juice, and Equal® in a bowl and mix well. Fill wafer cups with the fresh fruit.

Serves 12

NUTRITIONAL DATA

PER SERVING		EXCHANGES	
calories	184	milk	0.0
protein (gm)	2.0	vegetable	0.0
fat (gm)	1.8	fruit	2.0
cholesterol (mg)	3	bread	1.0
sodium (mg)	18	meat	0.0
% calories from fat	8	fat	0.0

♥

MOCHA-CRÈME-FILLED MERINGUE BASKETS

MOCHA CRÈME

1 cup non-fat dry milk

3 tablespoons cornstarch

2 tablespoons unsweetened cocoa

⅓ cup sugar, or 8 packets Equal®*

2 cups water

1 tablespoon instant coffee

1 teaspoon mocha extract

MERINGUE BASKETS

3 egg whites

⅛ teaspoon salt

¼ teaspoon cream of tartar

⅓ cup sugar

½ teaspoon mocha extract

Mocha Crème: Combine dry milk, cornstarch, cocoa, and sugar* in small saucepan. Stir well, and gradually stir in water mixed with instant coffee. Bring mixture to boil over medium heat, stirring constantly. Boil 2 minutes. Remove from heat and stir in mocha extract. Place mocha crème in plastic bowl with lid (this keeps a crust from forming). Chill.

Meringue Baskets: Preheat oven to 275°. Line baking sheet with wax paper.

Place egg whites in large bowl. Beat in mixer at medium speed until frothy. Add salt and cream of tartar. Beat on high speed until stiff. Slowly beat in sugar, a tablespoon at a time, beating with each addition. Beat in mocha extract.

Divide mixture into 6 equal parts, and drop onto prepared sheet, making mounds. Using a teaspoon, shape each mound into a circle 4 in. in diameter. Build up sides 1½ in. to make a basket. Bake 1 hour. Turn oven off and leave baskets in oven to cool. Do not open oven door.

To serve, place baskets on 6 individual serving plates. Mix mocha crème well and spoon into baskets, using ⅓ cup for each basket. Serve immediately. Meringues may be made a day ahead and stored in an airtight container until needed. Unfilled shells will keep several days.

Serves 6

NUTRITIONAL DATA

PER SERVING (using sugar)		EXCHANGES	
calories	152	milk	0.5
protein (gm)	6.2	vegetable	0.0
fat (gm)	0.3	fruit	0.0
cholesterol (mg)	2	bread	1.5
sodium (mg)	179	meat	0.0
% calories from fat	2	fat	0.0

♥

*Note: If using Equal®, add when you remove crème from heat and add the mocha extract.

PEACHES AND RASPBERRIES IN SPICED WINE

*I like to serve this dessert in elegant glass goblets.
A good use for those goblets you received as a
wedding gift or bought on an antique expedition.*

    1 bottle (750 ml) Italian dry white wine, such as Pinot
       Bianco

    ½ cup sugar, or 12 packets Equal®*

    4 ¾x2-in. orange peel strips (orange part only)

    3 cinnamon sticks

    6 peaches

    ½ pt. basket raspberries

Combine 1 cup wine, sugar*, orange peel, and cinnamon in small
saucepan. stir over low heat until sugar dissolves. Increase heat;
simmer 15 minutes. Remove from heat; add remaining wine.

Blanch peaches in large pot of boiling water 20 seconds. Transfer
to bowl of cold water, using slotted spoon. Drain. Pull off skin with
small knife. Slice peaches and transfer to large bowl. Add
raspberries and wine mixture.

Cover and refrigerate at least 1 hour; stir occasionally. (Can be
prepared 6 hours ahead.) Divide fruit and wine among glass goblets.

Serves 6

NUTRITIONAL DATA

PER SERVING (using sugar)		EXCHANGES	
calories	202	milk	0.0
protein (gm)	1.1	vegetable	0.0
fat (gm)	0.3	fruit	3.5
cholesterol (mg)	0	bread	0.0
sodium (mg)	6	meat	0.0
% calories from fat	1	fat	0.0

*Note: If using Equal®, add just before placing in refrigerator.

ITALIAN CHOCOLATE PUDDING CAKE*

1 cup all-purpose flour

¾ cup sugar

2 tablespoons Dutch cocoa

2 teaspoons baking powder

½ teaspoon salt

½ cup skim milk

2 tablespoons corn oil

1 teaspoon vanilla

Vegetable cooking spray

¾ cup brown sugar

¼ cup cocoa

1¾ cups hot water

Sift together flour, sugar, cocoa, baking powder, and salt. Add milk, oil, and vanilla, mixing well until smooth. Pour batter into an 8x8x2-in. baking pan sprayed with vegetable cooking spray. Combine brown sugar, cocoa, and water. Pour over batter. Bake at 350° for 45 minutes.

Serves 8

NUTRITIONAL DATA

PER SERVING		EXCHANGES	
calories	249	milk	0.0
protein (gm)	3.2	vegetable	0.0
fat (gm)	4.1	fruit	0.0
cholesterol (mg)	0	bread	3.0
sodium (mg)	231	meat	0.0
% calories from fat	15	fat	1.0

♥

*Note: This recipe is not recommended for people with diabetes because of its high sugar content.

GREEK DESSERTS

BAKED PEACH COMPOTE

3 lbs. (12–15) peaches, stoned
2 tablespoons fresh lemon juice
3 tablespoons mild-flavored honey
2 tablespoons currants
1 cup fresh blueberries
½ teaspoon ground ginger
½ teaspoon vanilla

Preheat oven to 350° degrees. Spray 2-qt. baking dish with vegetable cooking spray.

Blanch peaches in boiling water 20 seconds. Rinse under cold water and remove skins. Pit and slice. Toss with remaining ingredients in baking dish.

Bake in preheated oven 45 minutes to 1 hour. Serve warm or at room temperature. Compote will keep several days in refrigerator.

Serves 6

NUTRITIONAL DATA

PER SERVING		EXCHANGES	
calories	123	milk	0.0
protein (gm)	1.4	vegetable	0.0
fat (gm)	0.2	fruit	2.0
cholesterol (mg)	0	bread	0.0
sodium (mg)	2	meat	0.0
% calories from fat	2	fat	0.0

YOGURT ORANGE SORBET

2 5-oz. cartons plain, low-fat yogurt
1 6¼-oz. can concentrated orange juice
    Rind of 2 oranges, grated
¼ cup water
½ oz. (1½ tablespoons) gelatin
2 egg whites
2 oranges
2 tablespoons orange liqueur
    Orange peel curls for garnish

Mix yogurt, orange juice, and grated rind together in mixing bowl. Heat until hot, and stir in gelatin until it dissolves. Cool slightly, then add to yogurt mixture. Mix well, then put aside until syrupy and beginning to set.

Whisk egg whites until just stiff, then fold into yogurt mixture. Pour mixture into dish or cake tin and freeze until firm.

Peel oranges, removing all pith. Slice thinly and sprinkle with orange liqueur.

To serve, place layers of orange slices alternately with frozen sorbet, and decorate with curls of orange peel.

Serves 6

NUTRITIONAL DATA

PER SERVING		EXCHANGES	
calories	133	milk	1.0
protein (gm)	7.0	vegetable	0.0
fat (gm)	0.9	fruit	1.0
cholesterol (mg)	3	bread	0.0
sodium (mg)	55	meat	0.0
% calories from fat	6	fat	0.0

♥

SPANISH DESSERTS

FLAN*

*T*his *is Spain's most popular dessert. It is loved in Latin America, France, and most of the world. It can be served plain or topped with fresh fruit.*

1⅔ cups sugar (divided)
4 cups skim milk
  Rind of 1 orange, grated
1 teaspoon vanilla
  Egg substitute equal to 4 eggs

Place ⅔ cup sugar in small saucepan and cook until rich brown in color. Move pan constantly, and watch carefully so that sugar does not burn. Immediately pour caramel into 6 individual 1-cup custard cups or molds.

In large saucepan, bring milk to simmering point. Add remaining sugar and orange rind and simmer 5 minutes. Remove from heat and stir in vanilla. Let the milk stand several minutes, then beat in egg substitute.

Fill caramelized molds with custard and place in large pan of cold water. Bake in preheated 350° oven 35–40 minutes or until custard is set and lightly browned on top. Chill 4 hours in refrigerator. You can unmold custards on individual serving plates when ready to serve.

Serves 6

NUTRITIONAL DATA

PER SERVING		EXCHANGES	
calories	295	milk	1.0
protein (gm)	10.6	vegetable	0.0
fat (gm)	1.7	fruit	3.5
cholesterol (mg)	3	bread	0.0
sodium (mg)	159	meat	0.0
% calories from fat	5	fat	0.0

♥

*Note: This recipe is not recommended for people with diabetes because of its high sugar content.

SWEET RICE

T his dessert is nostalgic to many people and evokes thoughts of childhood to many.

   1 cup raw rice
   1 piece lemon rind
   2 cups water
1¾ cups evaporated skim milk
       Egg substitute equal to 2 eggs
   2 tablespoons sugar, or 2 packets Equal®*
   Cinnamon, ground, for garnish

Cook rice with lemon rind in 2 cups boiling water 15 minutes until almost tender. Drain rice and return to saucepan. Add milk, egg substitute, and sugar*, and simmer over low heat 1 hour. Place rice in serving dish and garnish with criss-cross pattern of ground cinnamon.
   Serves 4

NUTRITIONAL DATA

PER SERVING (using sugar)		EXCHANGES	
calories	305	milk	1.0
protein (gm)	15.5	vegetable	0.0
fat (gm)	1.6	fruit	0.0
cholesterol (mg)	5	bread	2.5
sodium (mg)	186	meat	1.0
% calories from fat	5	fat	0.0

***Note:** If using Equal®, add after placing rice in serving dish. Stir well and garnish with cinnamon.

MELON STUFFED WITH FRUIT AND FLOWERS

The idea for this dish came when teaching a garden class at a local cultural center. In these classes, I explain not only how to grow herbs and flowers but also how to use them in cooking. One morning the farmer's market offered wonderful melons, berries—and the largest nasturtium flowers I had ever seen! This quick and easy dessert resulted.

> 2 large cantaloupes
>
> 1 pt. raspberries
>
> 1 pt. blueberries
>
> 1 pt. strawberries
>
> 1 handful edible flowers, such as nasturtiums, rosemary, borage, or sage
>
> 6–8 tablespoons sugar, or 4 packets Equal®

Spoon fruit into melon shells. Arrange flowers among the berries. Sprinkle on sugar or sugar substitute. In hot weather, it is nice to serve the melons standing on beds of ice in shallow bowls.

Serves 4

NUTRITIONAL DATA

PER SERVING (using sugar)		EXCHANGES	
calories	287	milk	0.0
protein (gm)	4.4	vegetable	0.0
fat (gm)	1.8	fruit	4.5
cholesterol (mg)	0	bread	0.0
sodium (mg)	34	meat	0.0
% calories from fat	5	fat	0.0

MOROCCAN DESSERT

☆

BANANAS POACHED IN APPLE JUICE

2 cups apple juice
3 tablespoons raisins or currants
1 tablespoon vanilla extract
3-in. cinnamon stick
4 ripe bananas, peeled and sliced
Nutmeg, freshly grated
4-6 tablespoons non-fat yogurt

Combine apple juice, raisins or currants, vanilla, and cinnamon in saucepan and bring to simmer. Cook 5 minutes. Add bananas, cover, and simmer 8–10 minutes or just until bananas are tender. Remove cinnamon stick, sprinkle with nutmeg, and serve immediately with yogurt.

Serves 4

NUTRITIONAL DATA

PER SERVING		EXCHANGES	
calories	202	milk	0.0
protein (gm)	2.3	vegetable	0.0
fat (gm)	0.7	fruit	3.5
cholesterol (mg)	0	bread	0.0
sodium (mg)	17	meat	0.0
% calories from fat	3	fat	0.0

♥

BEVERAGES

FRENCH BEVERAGES

UN-CHAMPAGNE COCKTAIL

This is wonderful for entertaining; it should be made 5 or 6 hours in advance. You can double the recipe easily.

Peel of 1 orange

2 lumps sugar, or 2 packets Equal®

Angostura bitters

¼ cup cognac

3 bottles dry champagne

Wash and peel orange, carefully removing only the skin, not the pith. Put orange peel into cocktail shaker with sugar or Equal® (moistened with 3 dashes of Angostura bitters), add cognac and champagne, and mix.

Serves 15

NUTRITIONAL DATA

PER SERVING (with sugar)		EXCHANGES	
calories	120	milk	0.0
protein (gm)	0.3	vegetable	0.0
fat (gm)	0.0	fruit	2.0
cholesterol (mg)	0	bread	0.0
sodium (mg)	0	meat	0.0
% calories from fat	0	fat	0.0

♥

■

CAFÉ BRULOT

This after-dinner coffee has a spicy aroma and taste.

1 orange peel, with pith removed
2 cinnamon sticks, 3 in. long
20 whole cloves
3 cups water
4 teaspoons instant espresso
4 teaspoons brandy extract
Sugar substitute equal to 8 teaspoons sugar

Combine orange peel, cinnamon sticks, cloves, and water in 1½-qt. saucepan. Bring to boil and simmer, covered, 15 minutes. Remove from heat. Strain into 1-qt. container. Add instant espresso, brandy extract, and sugar substitute. Stir well. Pour into four 6-oz. coffee cups and serve.

Cold Variation: Chill before serving. Serve over 2 or 3 ice cubes in four 8-oz. glasses.

Serves 4

NUTRITIONAL DATA

PER SERVING		EXCHANGES	
calories	20	milk	0.0
protein (gm)	0.4	vegetable	0.0
fat (gm)	0.0	fruit	0.0
cholesterol (mg)	0	bread	0.0
sodium (mg)	2	meat	0.0
% calories from fat	0	fat	0.0

♥

TEA BRULOT

1 orange peel, with pith removed

2 cinnamon sticks, 3 in. long

20 whole cloves

3 cups water

4 tea bags

4 teaspoons rum extract

Sugar substitute equal to 8 teaspoons sugar

Combine orange peel, cinnamon sticks, cloves, and water in 1½-qt. saucepan. Bring to boil and simmer, covered, 15 minutes. Strain over 4 tea bags into 1-qt. container. (Or add 4 teaspoons instant unsweetened tea.) Add rum extract and sugar substitute. Stir well. Pour into four 6-oz. teacups and serve.

Cold Variation: Chill before serving. Serve over 2 or 3 ice cubes in four 8-oz. glasses.

Serves 4

NUTRITIONAL DATA

PER SERVING		EXCHANGES	
calories	13	milk	0.0
protein (gm)	0.0	vegetable	0.0
fat (gm)	0.0	fruit	0.0
cholesterol (mg)	0	bread	0.0
sodium (mg)	0	meat	0.0
% calories from fat	0	fat	0.0

ITALIAN BEVERAGES

CAPPUCCINO

You can make cappuccino without a cappuccino machine by whipping warm milk in a blender for 1 minute to produce a bit of foam. Combine equal quantities of very strong, freshly brewed, Italian-roast coffee with the frothy milk. Dust with chocolate shavings and ground cinnamon, and serve with sugar or a sugar substitute.

ICED ESPRESSO

A rich-tasting coffee drink with a hint of chocolate. This is an excellent replacement for dessert.

  4 tablespoons cocoa

  2 cups espresso coffee, either instant or brewed

  3 cups skim milk

  Sugar substitute equal to 4 tablespoons sugar

15–20 ice cubes

Place cocoa and espresso in 2-qt. saucepan and cook until hot, beating to a froth with wire whisk or hand eggbeater. Add skim milk and beat until mixture is frothy. Remove from heat. Add sugar substitute. Refrigerate, covered, to room temperature. Place 3 ice cubes in each of five 10-oz. glasses. Pour mixture over ice cubes.

  Serves 7

NUTRITIONAL DATA

PER SERVING		EXCHANGES	
calories	52	milk	0.5
protein (gm)	4.4	vegetable	0.0
fat (gm)	0.6	fruit	0.0
cholesterol (mg)	2	bread	0.0
sodium (mg)	56	meat	0.0
% calories from fat	10	fat	0.0

♥

SPICY HOT COCOA

2 cinnamon sticks, about 3 in. long

8 whole cloves

¾ cup skim milk

2 teaspoons cocoa

2 teaspoons hot water

Sugar substitute to taste

Place cinnamon sticks, cloves, and skim milk in small saucepan. Heat slowly, bringing mixture to just below boiling point. Set aside.

Place cocoa and hot water in small saucepan. Mix. Heat to boiling. Stir constantly to dissolve. Boil 1 minute. Remove from heat, and add cocoa to milk and spice mixture. Strain. Sweeten to taste. Pour drink into an 8-oz. mug.

Serves 1

NUTRITIONAL DATA

PER SERVING		EXCHANGES	
calories	73	milk	1.0
protein (gm)	7.1	vegetable	0.0
fat (gm)	0.8	fruit	0.0
cholesterol (mg)	3	bread	0.0
sodium (mg)	95	meat	0.0
% calories from fat	10	fat	0.0

GREEK BEVERAGES

DIOSMO

Diosmo, or "double mint," is the morning drink of choice for many Greeks. It is calorie free!

6 teaspoons dried mint

6 cups water

Boil dried mint in water. Strain and serve.
Serves 6

NUTRITIONAL DATA

PER SERVING		EXCHANGES	
calories	0	milk	0.0
protein (gm)	0.0	vegetable	0.0
fat (gm)	0.0	fruit	0.0
cholesterol (mg)	0	bread	0.0
sodium (mg)	0	meat	0.0
% calories from fat	0	fat	0.0

FASCOMILO
(Sage Tea)

6 cups water

12 teaspoons dried sage

Bring water to boil and add sage. Cover and let stand 5–7 minutes before serving.

Serves 6

NUTRITIONAL DATA

PER SERVING		EXCHANGES	
calories	0	milk	0.0
protein (gm)	0.0	vegetable	0.0
fat (gm)	0.0	fruit	0.0
cholesterol (mg)	0	bread	0.0
sodium (mg)	0	meat	0.0
% calories from fat	0	fat	0.0

SPANISH BEVERAGES

SANGRIA

3 oranges

1 lemon

3 cloves

½ cup confectioner's sugar, or 12 packets Equal®

3 qts. red wine

3 oranges, sliced thin, for garnish

Wash oranges and lemon and cut into thin slices. Place in large glass pitcher, add cloves and sugar or Equal®, cover with wine. Place in refrigerator to chill until time to serve.

Before serving, stir, and place ice cubes in glasses. Garnish with orange slices.

Makes about 3 quarts.

Serves 12

NUTRITIONAL DATA

PER SERVING (using sugar)		EXCHANGES	
calories	184	milk	0.0
protein (gm)	0.5	vegetable	0.0
fat (gm)	0.0	fruit	3.0
cholesterol (mg)	0	bread	0.0
sodium (mg)	12	meat	0.0
% calories from fat	0	fat	0.0

GAZPACHO DRINK

*This drink is a gorgeous red color, and it's spicy,
like the traditional soup. Make it a few hours
before serving to chill well.*

¼ cup green onions and onion tops, cut into pieces
1 medium cucumber, peeled and diced (1 cup)
1 medium bell pepper, cut up (1 cup)
1 clove garlic, minced
2 tablespoons tarragon vinegar
4 dashes hot pepper sauce
½ teaspoon Spike
Dash red food coloring
4 celery sticks for garnish

Place all ingredients except celery sticks in blender and blend thoroughly. If blender jar is not large enough, blend in small batches, and transfer drink to 1-qt. pitcher.

Refrigerate, covered, to chill for several hours. Pour into four 8-oz. or larger glasses. Use celery sticks for garnish.

Serves 4

NUTRITIONAL DATA

PER SERVING		EXCHANGES	
calories	22	milk	0.0
protein (gm)	1.0	vegetable	1.0
fat (gm)	0.2	fruit	0.0
cholesterol (mg)	0	bread	0.0
sodium (mg)	37	meat	0.0
% calories from fat	7	fat	0.0

♥

MOROCCAN BEVERAGE

MINT TEA

In Morocco, making mint tea is a highly formalized art. The host usually makes the tea at the end of a meal, often with great ceremony.

Boiling water

1½ tablespoons green tea

1 handful fresh mint leaves and stalks

Sugar to taste

Rinse out a 3-cup teapot with hot water. Add tea. Pour in ½ cup boiling water, swish around quickly, and empty water (leaving tea in pot). This is supposed to remove any bitterness from the tea.

Stuff mint leaves and stalks into pot and add sugar. Fill pot with boiling water. Let steep 5–8 minutes, checking occasionally to be sure mint doesn't rise above the water. Stir, taste, and add sugar if necessary. Serve traditionally in small glasses set in silver holders.

Serves 3

NUTRITIONAL DATA

PER SERVING		EXCHANGES	
calories	6	milk	0.0
protein (gm)	0.0	vegetable	0.0
fat (gm)	0.0	fruit	0.0
cholesterol (mg)	0	bread	0.0
sodium (mg)	5	meat	0.0
% calories from fat	0	fat	0.0

MENUS FOR HOLIDAYS AND SPECIAL OCCASIONS

New Year's Dinner

Bruschetta, p. 16
Gazpacho, Drink, p. 290
Chicken Piccata, p. 75
Zucchini Italiano, p. 132
Cherries Jubilee, p. 259

Super Bowl Sunday

Artichoke Dip, p. 23
Hummus, p. 20
Pizza Primavera, p. 191
Potato-Crusted Pizza, p. 187
Italian Chocolate Pudding Cake,
    p. 272

Mardi Gras Celebration

Garlic Soup, p. 33
Mushroom Salad, p. 53
Loin of Pork in Wine Sauce, p. 102
Artichoke Delight, p. 127
Bread Pudding with Raisins and
    Bourbon Sauce, pp. 254, 249

Valentine's Dinner for Two

Asparagus Provençal, p. 5
Beef Sirloin Béarnaise, p. 91
Carrots Vichy, p. 126
Lemon, Cucumber, and Bell
    Pepper Salad, p. 49
Coeur à la Crème, p. 262

Easter

Minestrone, p. 32
Lisbon Salad, p. 59
Kapama (Chicken with Spices),
    p. 76
Rosemary-Scented Potato Gratin,
    p. 124
Mocha-Crème-Filled Meringue
    Baskets, p. 269

Mother's Day Brunch

Peaches and Raspberries in Spiced
    White Wine, p. 271
Vegetable Flan, p. 9
Lentil and Rice Pilaf, p. 152
Shrimp with Feta Cheese, p. 117
String Bean Salad, p. 57
Chocolate Madeleines, p. 252

Father's Day Luncheon

Italian Mushroom Soup, p. 34
Chicken Saltimbocca, p. 74
Pasta with Wild Mushrooms, Peas,
    and Dried Tomatoes, p. 168
Tomato and Cucumber Salad with
    Fresh Basil, p. 60
Pears in Red Wine, p. 266

Here Comes the Bride

Endive Leaves with Ratatouille, p. 6
Rice Malgache, p. 141
Chicken Dijon, p, 66
Tante Marie's Tossed Green Salad,
    p. 48
Wafer Cups with Fresh Fruit, p. 268

Country French Picnic

Stuffed Tomatoes and Green
    Peppers, p. 206
Pinchitos (Lamb Kabobs with
    Spicy Lemon Sauce), 103
Moroccan Carrot Salad, p. 63
Couscous with Seven Vegetables,
    p. 157
Bananas Poached in Apple Juice,
    p. 279

Halloween

Marinated Artichoke Hearts and
    Peppers, p. 12
Provençal Pizza, p. 182
Pizza Rustica, p. 185
Stuffed Pumpkin, p. 197
Lemon, Cucumber, and Bell
    Pepper Salad, p. 49
Apple Tart Tatin, p. 263

Pastas with Panache

Italian Antipasto, p. 11
Pasta with Creamy Pesto, p. 164
Pasta with Fresh Seafood Sauce,
    p. 166
Pasta with Tomato, Eggplant, and
    Bell Pepper Sauce, p. 163
Classic Greek Salad, p. 56
Pèches Melba, p. 256

Christmas Eve

Artichokes with Green Sauce, p. 22
Paella Valenciana, p. 154
Salad Niçoise, p. 46
Flan, p. 275

INDEX